FURNITURE
REPAIR AND CONSTRUCTION
Styles, restoring and projects — Step by step

IDEA BOOKS

FURNITURE, REPAIR AND BUILDING

© **IDEA BOOKS, S.A.**
Rosellón, 186, 1º. 4ª
08008 Barcelona –Spain– Tel. 34 3 4533002
http://www.ideabooks.es/

Book management / **Juan B. Lorente Herrera**
Editing / **Anna Garcia Pascual**
Artistic creation and drawings / **Lluis Lladó Teixidó**
Restoration projects / **Concepción Font Flinch**
Technical restorer / **Silvia Guix Font**
Photography / **Angel Barambio**
Archive photography / **Alfa Omega**
and **Idea Books**
Translation / **abc Traduccions**
Photomechanics / **BCN**
Printing / **Rol press**

We would like to thank the following companies for
their creations and help given in this book:
Eduardo Terradez (cover photo)
Bosch (tools)
Ateliers Geka (introduction)
Epoca (furniture)
3M Spain (abrasives)

EDITION 1998 Legal Deposit B–161–98
ISBN 84–8236–036–2

CONTENTS

1/ INTRODUCTION

2/ STYLES

3/ RESTORATION PROJECT
(step-by-step)

4/ ASSEMBLIES

5/ RESTORATION AND REPAIR

6/ FINISHES AND DECORATIONS

7/ WORKSHOP AND TOOLS

8/ WOODS

9/ VARNISHES

10/ PAINTS

11/ CONSTRUCTION

12/ ANALYTICAL INDEX

INTRODUCTION

This book is primarily aimed at anyone wishing to keep pieces of furniture and objects dating from previous generations or cultures in the best possible condition, thereby enhancing their enjoyment of them. It is, however, also directed at anyone wishing to get rid of the marks left behind as a legacy of everyday use, as well as those arising from the inevitable "accidents" these objects suffer in the home.

Now, you don't have to be a professional to do this, simply follow the practical, safe instructions as given in this guide and repairing, restoring or making the majority of furniture will be problem-free. Obviously, some jobs will need a great deal of patience, plus a certain level of manual skill which does come with practice. When the piece of furniture is of great value or very old, it is best to consult an experienced specialist or professional prior to using it or carrying out any repair or restoration work whatsoever on it. Very often, there are differences of opinion between the very same experts as to what treatment has to be applied when restoring furniture to be exhibited in museums.

Nowadays, the general consensus is to strictly "conserve" what has lasted up to our times and to simply apply the most suitable treatment to ensure that deterioration stops, but without replacing damaged parts or putting on a new finish over the original, let alone replacing it completely or completing lost component parts.

1

2

The restoration dealt with in this book has a different goal; in the case in question, pieces of furniture, the aim is to return them to their original appearance, giving them back their original charm, always with a view to installing them in a home where they will be "used" and not just be there as decoration, aside from the sentimental or historical value they may have. On the whole, it is necessary to differentiate between "Restore," "Repair" and "Conserve."

For those pieces of historical value and which are kept in museums as testimony to ages past, the best restorers are of the opinion that it is best to simply "conserve" what is left of the pieces which, in some cases, are very deteriorated:

Furniture. Repair and making clean, strengthen if need be, stick what has come loose or stop an infestation of woodworm or dry rot but never, repeat never, paint or touch up the finish nor replace deteriorated parts for new ones. Experts usually say that there are more historical treasures lost by improper or disrespectful restoration than those lost as a result of the passage of time and atmospheric vicissitudes.

When speaking of "repairing," what is meant is sticking or repairing but without retouching, painting or trying to make the repair blend in seamlessly. "Restoration" is done as an overall job, including new parts, paintwork, finishes, etc. The objective is to return the piece to its original appearance and charm, bearing in mind that it will now be installed in a home where it is expected to be of use aside from simply giving of its beauty and historical interest. Included in the restorer's ethics is the point of not doing any repair work which may mislead the purchaser or owner, hiding a fault, defect or making it appear older than what it really is so as to change its face value. However, the dust of deterioration and dirt are entirely different materia altogether, and everything is improved with careful cleaning. One rule to follow in all cases is: to stop the ravages of time by using all those treatments which offset or repair any damage caused by woodworm, dry rot, etc. Pieces of furniture may also be restored which do not have any historical or artistic value, but which with a few modifications, the right treatment, a different finish or more attractive decoration, thereby give it a beauty it lacked beforehand.

The first task of the restorer, both professional and amateur alike, will be to carefully inspect the piece prior to undertaking any treatment or repair, to chiefly confirm its value or lack of it, and thus work accordingly.

Some cabinetmakers, and even manufacturers, used to sign their works, engrave their initials and date them or put their seal on some part or other of them. These signs have great significance, given that they may play a decisive role in deciding the piece's value –dating it properly or authenticating its origin. These signs could be anywhere on the piece, very often not immediately visible; on the bottom or back of a drawer, under the top of a desk or table or on the inside of a leg.... often as not, it is worked into the decoration on a border or motif... A sign of this kind could mean that the piece is then recognised as a valuable object and deserving of the finest

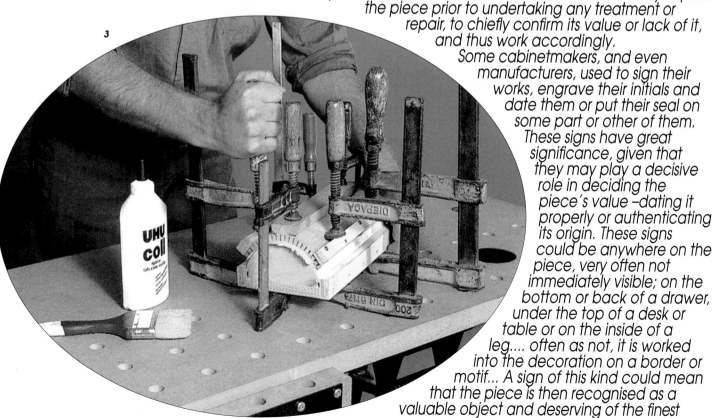

4

3

professional attention ... not any different to those given in this book. The main difference arises from the experience and authority of the professional restorer, who has handled innumerable valuable pieces. When deciding to restore a piece of furniture without any historical or artistic value, freedom of choice is obviously much greater: you can change its appearance radically, changing the paintwork or colour, adding or modifying decoration, even the size. There are pieces of furniture which just do not go in a modern home or wardrobes in which you'd like to keep other things, etc. When entering an antique shop, the vast majority of the objects and pieces of furniture on display there are already restored and, despite the lack of space usually the norm in this kind of locale, properly installed to form small settings in which each piece of furniture or object in shown to its best advantage, thereby enhancing those in its immediate surrounds. Contrariwise, when entering a warehouse where everything is bundled together and covered in dust, it is doubly difficult to chose a piece of furniture ... but, once restored by our own efforts and to our taste, will give much greater pleasure when contemplated and used.

5

1/ However magnificent the machinery, it is still necessary to manually finish it with artisanal skill to give a perfect carving.

2/ The careful choice of woodgrain on the veneer of this sideboard is enhanced with the citrus wood border.

3/ In order to make sticking of the veneer perfect, a 3 mm thick multi-laminate wood veneer is adapted to the mould with cramp frames.

4/ Writing desk with two drawers and folding top. The legs are truncated inverted pyramid shaped, ending in a butt.

5/ The marquetry of this low table's top reproduces the pattern of the parquet flooring at Fontainebleau.

6/ There are pieces the diameter of which makes them impossible to achieve. Careful study of the woodgrain and gluing will give a perfect finish.

6

FURNITURE STYLES

Knowledge of the history of art and the evolution in furniture making throughout the different historical periods, as well as the most commonly used techniques in each epoch and country, can greatly help when deciding on the possible value of a piece. There are, however, a great many other objects and pieces of furniture which are of very little intrinsic value though they are antiques, these pieces of furniture are those which, after careful cleaning and restoration, will gain in attractiveness and become useful in whatever setting they are put. There are also pieces of furniture which can only be considered as "ugly" to whom a good finish, perhaps a more cheerful decoration, the renovation of the upholstery or the addition of a grecque or moulding, will make them more attractive in appearance.

At the gates of the 21st century, there are still a great many pieces of furniture dating from end of the 19th century and beginning of the 20th which are gaining in value and interest almost daily, even much maligned "functional" pieces from the fifties and sixties have a design and originality which new generations will appreciate in every increasing droves. They are pieces of furniture which will probably need one or more parts renovating or replacing.

The sum total of the stylisation of many of their component parts has made them more fragile than those more solidly made appertaining to previous epochs. This very problem is the selfsame one presented by authentic pieces of furniture of the Rococo or Empire style. It must also be borne in mind that the authentic restorer will not only get enjoyment out of the results obtained, but will also take pride in carrying out each one of the steps comprising the slow process to be followed and eventually reach a satisfactory conclusion.

Dividing the history of furniture up broadly from the Renaissance epoch (roughly between the 14th and 15th centuries according to the different European countries), given that it is highly improbable that a piece antedating this time will fall into our hands, will give us some extensive furniture groups which, aside from their general lines, will also be divided up according to their construction and ornamentation.

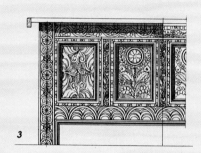

1/ Characteristic melon bulb from the English Renaissance.

2/ English Renaissance sideboard, decorated with Tudor rose and other carvings (1689).

3/ Renaissance carving on a chest from the English Renaissance (Esther/Hobsonne, dated 1637).

Group 1

ENGLISH RENAISSANCE – FRENCH RENAISSANCE (Louis XIII) – SPANISH RENAISSANCE

English Renaissance. The arrival of this epoch produced several furniture styles which came one hard on the heels of the other their characteristics, however, off-repeated in all of them though there were some differentiating traits, it must be said. These styles are comprised of the Tudor, Elizabethan, Jacobean, Cromwellian, Restoration and Late Jacobean. In the first three, the decorative details which are repeated over and over again are: the Tudor rose carved on panels, corners, etc., and the large-sized melon bulb of plain proportions or richly decorated on the turning of legs. The tendency in the latter three styles is toward a greater sobriety insofar as decoration, but with the emphasis on a careful finish and balanced proportions. One of the characteristic principles is that the first pieces of furniture appeared where the quintessential element was user comfort and not the ostentation of its dignity or richness.

French Renaissance (Louis XIII). *In France –Italy too– furniture was characterised by a much more horizontal structure than preceding epochs, aligned with great technical advances in the finishing and polishing of woods, walnut on the whole. Cabinetmaking, marquetry and bronze were introduced for decoration, in addition to carvings which were the sole decorative element in previous epochs.*
The structure is composed of the joined pieces which form one whole unit. The sizes and architectural decorative fronts are superimposed on the structure.

4/ Wardrobe–sideboard from the French Renaissance (reign of Henry II).

5/ Richly carved table from the French Renaissance (Henry III).

6/ Typical chair from the Spanish Renaissance (ca 1600).

7/ Fragment of a Portuguese bureau (second half of 16th century).

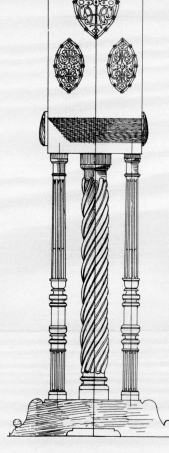

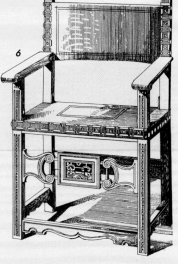

Spanish Renaissance. *Though there are large differences between the north of the country –influenced by France– the Levant more influenced by dealings with Italy, and the south where the Arabic influence is very deeply entrenched, the use of iron is nevertheless extremely commonplace everywhere, used to strengthen structures and for the inlay work with Moorish motifs to a greater or lesser extent.*
The most original piece of furniture is the decorated Spanish cabinet which is still built even today. For the rest of the pieces of furniture: the sturdily moulded coffers, tiles and balustrades, the rich turnings and thick cuts are characteristic of all of them.

13
·······

GENERAL CONSTRUCTION AND ORNAMENTATION CHARACTERISTICS

These are usually made out of solid wood and generally simple (wood–wood for joining the different parts of the piece), and fixed using nails or suchlike implements. Proportioned rather rectilinear shapes, excepting large–sized carvings. Abundant inlay work, carved, etc. decoration. Legs generally turned or with a gentle cabriolet effect.

Group 2

LOUIS XIV and LOUIS XV – FURNITURE FROM ENGLAND, HOLLAND, THE LOW COUNTRIES AND GERMANY – THE BAROQUE IN SPAIN AND PORTUGAL

Louis XIV and Louis XV. *On a par with the importance of the English styles in the previous group, in this epoch the greater influence was exercised by French taste for furniture. Majestic, overpowering proportions, richly decorated, symmetry, curved lines and upholstered seats, all characterise the pieces of furniture from the reign of Louis XIV. The Louis XV or Rococo style looks for a certain symmetry in the lines and together with the decoration gives the piece of furniture a special gracefulness. If Louis XIV furniture is luxurious and solemn, that of the Rococo is delicate, graceful and of exquisite taste.*

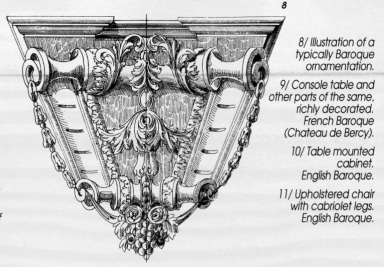

8/ Illustration of a typically Baroque ornamentation.

9/ Console table and other parts of the same, richly decorated. French Baroque (Chateau de Bercy).

10/ Table mounted cabinet. English Baroque.

11/ Upholstered chair with cabriolet legs. English Baroque.

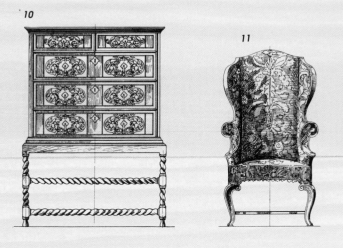

English, Dutch, Low Country and German furniture. *Not many changes here though better working becoming the norm. On the whole, the furniture is more ornate than the French pieces, but more solid, decorative and well–finished.*
In both England (William and Mary or Queen Anne style) and France, the crosspieces strengthening the legs of chairs are now being phased out and are instead being fitted with needlework upholstery to make them more comfortable on the back and seat. At the end of this epoch, Chippendale, the first creator of furniture to have his name applied to a style other than that of a monarch, appeared in the United Kingdom. The most characteristic point of this style are the chairs produced in multiple forms and tendencies; influenced by the Gothic, Chinese and many other styles, but always harmonious and of great beauty.

The Baroque in Spain and Portugal. *The main characteristic of Baroque furniture in these countries and their overseas colonies consists of the abundance and richness of the turnings. Some original designs were created such as the "Lyre table" (comprised of an elegant metal frame design used to strengthen the union between legs and top), other models of decorated Spanish cabinet and the introduction of usage of one of the exotic woods most solicited up to our time: mahogany.*
The exuberant architecture of Churriguera also influenced the decoration of the panels and legs of the pieces of furniture.

12

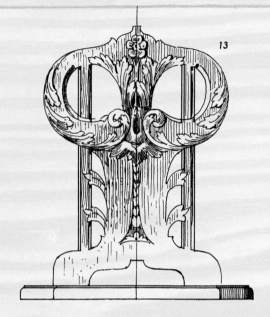

13

12/ Richly carved Baroque cabinet. The wreathed columns are seated on the lower, broader section.

13/ Carved back of Baroque chair (German Baroque).

14/ The turning on the legs of this German Baroque table is outstanding.

14

GENERAL CONSTRUCTION AND ORNAMENTATION CHARACTERISTICS
•••••••••••••••••••••••••••••••••••

Elegant gracious forms on the curves, made basically by carving large pieces of hardwoods. Cabriolet legs in almost all cases. Different parts of the furniture assembled using complicated methods than previously used (tenon, dovetail, hidden pegs, etc.) Decorative motifs somewhat simpler but more refined. Inlay work or finishes in metal, semi–precious stones, exotic hardwoods, etc. On the Louis XV furniture, the cabinetmaker's art reached its zenith. This multiplication of the abovementioned joins had one sole aim, to make invisible the joins between the different pieces, trying to achieve lines and curves in horizontal and, in particular, on those vertical components. The cabriolet legs are omnipresent and are designed to achieve maximum stylisation effect.

Group 3

LOUIS XVI, NEOCLASSIC, EMPIRE AND CONSULATE–ADAM HEPPLEWHITE, TRAFALGAR AND QUEEN VICTORIA

Louis XVI, Neoclassic, Empire and Consulate. In France and likewise in the rest of the European countries and Americas, a reaction to the exaggeration of the curves from forerunner styles took place, bringing about a return to the classical (or to what was then taken as this), in both architecture and furniture alike: the Neoclassical style or Louis XVI.
Legs once again became straight, but now much finer and frequently shaped like the trunk of an inverted pyramid, or sometimes circular section and turned. Furniture is painted in pastel shades with gilding reserved for filets or small motifs.
The Director and Consulate styles adhered to these tendencies, the major differences here being the decorative motifs (Egyptian influence arising out of Napoleon's campaign there: caryatids, gryphons, winged genii, etc., gilded bronze appliques; laurel wreaths, bees and other allegorical motifs of triumph and industry).

15/ Legs on Neoclassical furniture are stylised but without giving up being richly decorated.

16/ Neoclassical table decorated with carvings and inlay work.

17/ Classicism in design, the stylisation of form and the delicacy of execution are evident in this Louis XVI table leg.

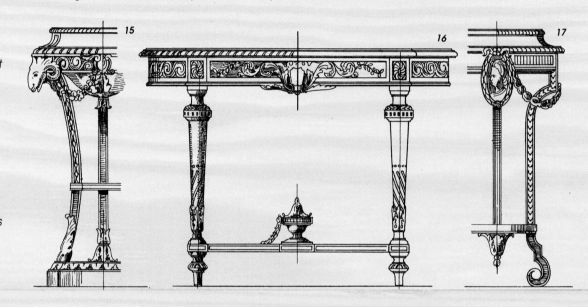

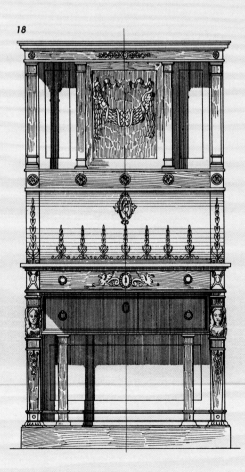

18/ Another interpretation of classical motifs on this French Empire style bureau.

19/ Louis XVI style ornamental motif.

20/ A voluted tripod and column form the support for many tables dating from this epoch.

Adam and Hepplewhite, Trafalgar and Queen Victoria.

Round this same epoch in England there was a social change and furniture became more widespread without losing its quality. The craftsmen Adam and Hepplewhite were some such artisans, the creators of well–designed furniture exhibiting good taste with a mixture of curved and straight lines. Very similar to the Empire style but with motifs alluding to the Victorian naval might of that time, this being the Trafalgar style.

Many of these pieces of furniture exhibit a clearly seen trend dating from the preceding epoch but which continues and gains ground in this one: the Oriental influence with the insertion of Chinese and Japanese lacquers on European furniture, as well as on auxiliary furniture from India, Arabia, etc.

In reaction a new Rococo of sorts appeared, called the Louis Philippe style in France, Queen Victoria in England and Isabelline in Spain, and shortly thereafter, Governing Queen. Throughout all of Europe the influences emanating from these two countries – England and France– who played greater roles in politics though each country continued to produce furniture in its own style with particular national characteristics.

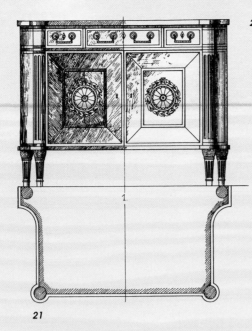

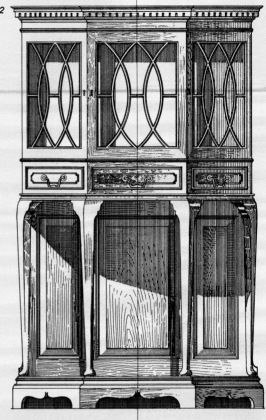

21/ Adam style chest of drawers as an expression of Neoclassicism in England.

22/ English Hepplewhite sideboard (the pattern formed by the latticework in the glass is highly characteristic).

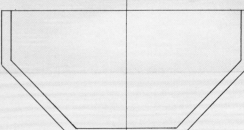

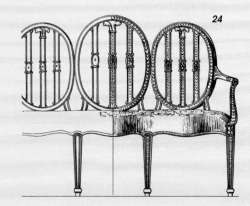

23/ Adam style chest of drawers, decorated front and semi–circular in shape.

24/ Three–seater English seat (Adam).

17

GENERAL CONSTRUCTION AND ORNAMENTATION CHARACTERISTICS

In the Louis XVI style, a return is made to the classical sobriety of straight lines and moderate proportions. The decorative elements are taken for classic Greek and Roman architecture. In the Empire style, some characteristic ornamental motifs (bees, Napoleon's initial and others reminiscent of furniture painting and architecture from the Egyptian civilisation arising from the Napoleonic campaign there) are the main highlights, in conjunction with the use of exotic hardwoods, mahogany in particular.

Group 4
FEDERAL, WINDSOR, AMERICAN, ETC.

Thanks to international trade, exotic woods became ever-increasingly more available and much easier to get in all countries: furniture and fashion are no longer the exclusive preserves of royal families, the upper and middle class families now had salons, dining rooms, dressing rooms, offices, etc. The American styles appertain to this epoch: Federal, American Windsor, etc.

After the fall of Napoleon and during the Second Empire, fashion trends came hard on the heels of each other and during the different decades of the 19th century industrially made furniture became more commonly available and widespread, replacing the painstakingly made furniture built by craftsmen in a small workshop.

This industrialisation had an effect on the quality of the furniture, but did favour its extension amongst the lower social classes, the end result being that there are still a lot of examples existing dating back from that epoch around today.

With the Romanticism and subsequently the Biedermeier styles (Germany), Arts and Crafts (England), Art Nouveau (France), Modern Style, etc., trends which in Spain gave birth to Modernism.

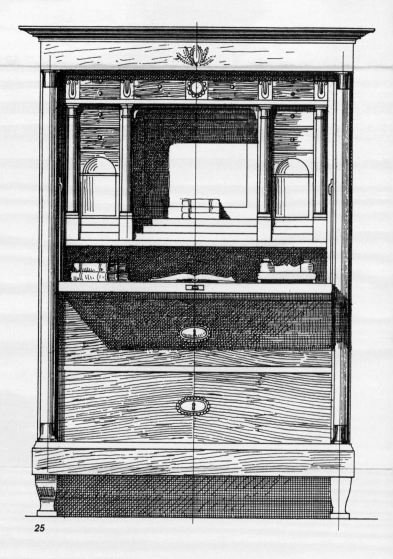

25/ Biedermeier style bureau.

26/ Bed conserving the Empire style's lines but which, for decorative reasons is decidedly Biedermeier style.

25

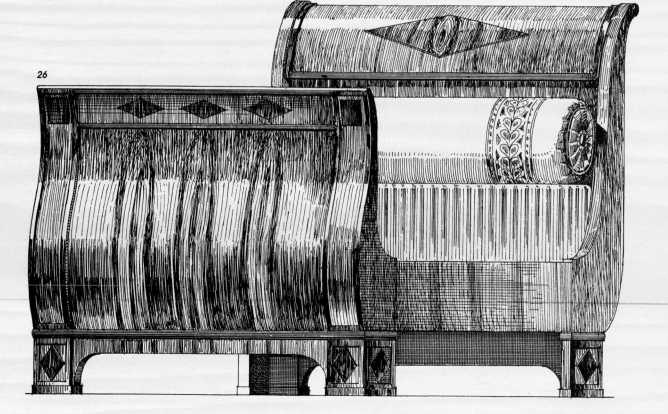

26

27/ Divan made following the design dictates of the Biedermeier style.

28/ Three–seater seat, Biedermeier style.

29/ Round table, Biedermeier style. (Tiefurt Castle, near to Weimar).

30/ Biedermeier style armchair. Seat and upper section of the back, lightly upholstered.

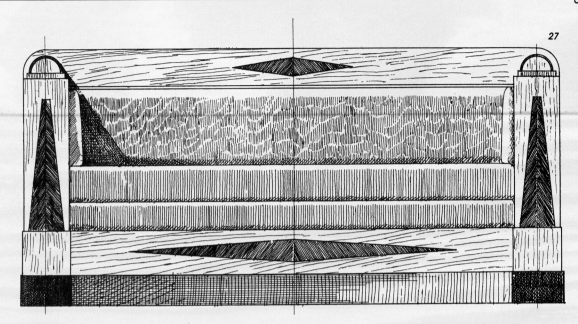

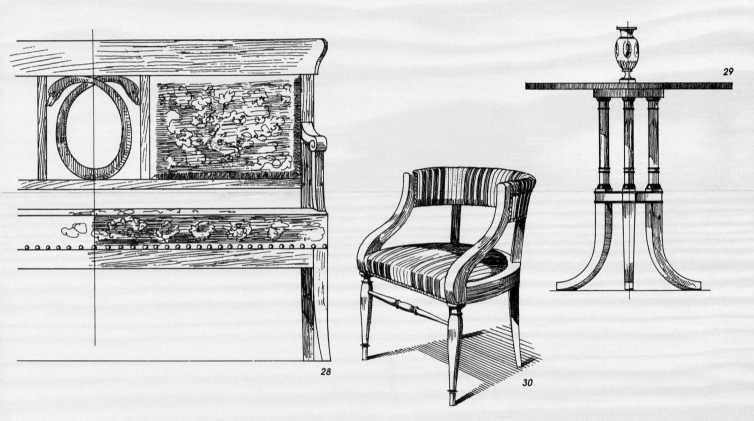

19

GENERAL CONSTRUCTION AND ORNAMENTATION CHARACTERISTICS

In keeping with the passing of the century, the Romanticism trend introduced the return to Middle age aesthetical ideals into architecture and, in particular, furniture design. With a peculiar imitation not of the furniture of that time but of the characteristics of the Gothic architecture, passing it over to the world of furniture. The same thing happened with all the subsequent epochs and styles. Frequently found amongst this furniture are seats either upholstered or covered by raffia, cane, etc., with hangings, curtains and tapestries abounding in houses. All kinds of adornments are used: carvings, bronzes, inlay work, marquetry, etc. Furniture is almost entirely veneered and the grain of the exotic woods is set out so as to form pretty patterns. Probably these or still later ones, will be the furniture coming into the hands of the restorer and reader of this very book, who will want to get into taking care of the furniture of their parents, grandparents or those so joyfully discovered in auctions, clearance sales or flea markets.

Group 5

ARTS & CRAFTS, MODERNISM, CUBISM, ETC.

Began at the beginning of the previous century, in the first years of the 20th century and right up to the twenties and thirties, reaching their zenith then, were the Arts and Crafts, Modernism, Cubism, etc. movements, forecasting a return to the "well–made" product the hallmark of which was a detailed study of austere straight or slightly curved lines. (A section apart should be given over to the furniture designed by Gaudi and which are still kept and preserved today in museums and historical buildings).
Belonging to the second half of the 20th century now drawing to a close, these pieces of furniture began some decades before and were called "design" or "functional" pieces. They are pieces of furniture which cannot be strictly classed as antiques, but which have merit enough to appropriately restored and kept.

31/ Simplicity of lines and careful construction.

32/ Assembled structure and ergonomic design of writing desk.

31

32

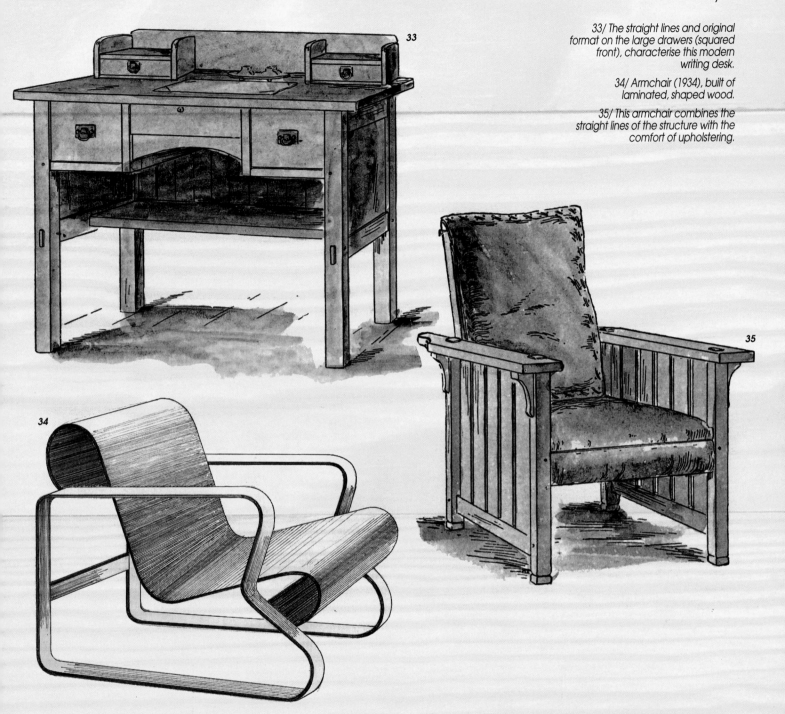

33/ The straight lines and original format on the large drawers (squared front), characterise this modern writing desk.

34/ Armchair (1934), built of laminated, shaped wood.

35/ This armchair combines the straight lines of the structure with the comfort of upholstering.

GENERAL CONSTRUCTION AND ORNAMENTATION CHARACTERISTICS

Generally made in series or by craftsmen who make use of all the facilities offered by the new machinery continually being perfected and automating production.
The furniture's beauty is based on its lines, comfort and usefulness it offers in line with its pure styling without losing sight of the possibility of production in series and widespread distribution in the ever increasing universal market.
The bright colours, the use of new finishes based on products derived from petroleum, plus the new materials which very often also have their roots in the black gold of this century. Steel (already used in the 19th century for furniture which today enjoys great historical and artistic standing), and other metals are also considered as suitable materials for making furniture.
Modern products also enjoy great importance in some treatments and care, thereby avoiding their deterioration or infestation.
Great care must always be taken before applying them or replacing a damaged finish, remember that improper restoration will almost certainly wipe out the value of a singular, unique piece.

Group 6
RUSTIC FURNITURE

While the history of furniture was being developed in the Royal courts, palaces of the nobility and the homes of the upper classes, furniture also played an important role in the furnishing of simple folk's homes who enjoyed a certain level of economic sufficiency. The trends set by the capitals were followed, though this lagged behind the capital's current mode as was to be expected, more weight being given to the sturdiness of the furniture than to the exquisiteness of its design. Using much simpler materials and not so highly skilled craftsmen, the resulting furniture had a distinct bearing. This is the furniture of the French Provincial style (Provençal, Normandy, etc.), Nordic furniture and that from central Europe (Hungary, the Black Forest, Tyrol, etc.)

36/ Rustic style chair with arms (end 18th century).

37/ Rustic chair with crosspiece back (end 18th century).

38/ Sideboard with glass display cabinet forming the upper section (Lausitz, 1802).

39/ Grandfather clock. Housed in Moritzburg (ca 1800).

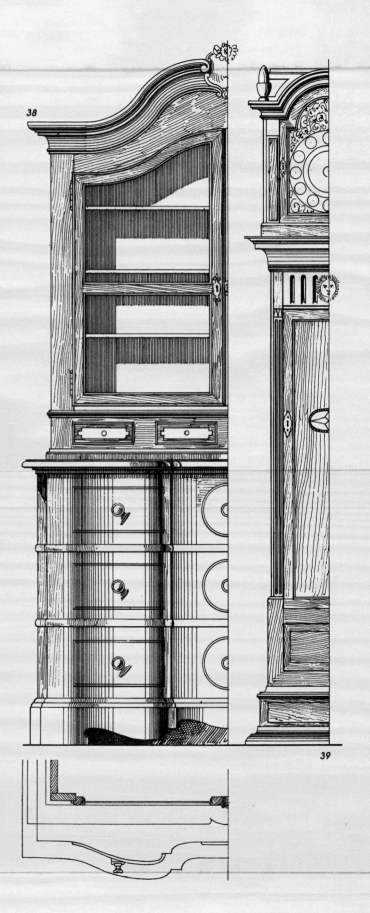

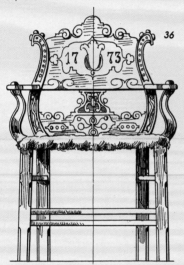

40/ *Rustic style wardrobe, double doors with drawers in the bottom section,*
decorated with flowers and dating from 1797. (Vogtland).

41/ *Rustic style sideboard or chest of drawers (1793)*

GENERAL CONSTRUCTION AND
ORNAMENTATION CHARACTERISTICS

These are pieces of furniture which very often are made entirely by hand or with very simple tools.
The carvings are rustic in nature. Polished using wax or oil and decorated with bright, happy colours. The most frequently used motifs
are flowers alternating with the fauna found in the forests forming the countryside of the craftsman.

EVOLUTION OF THE STYLES IN DIFFERENT COMPONENT PARTS

This brief overview of the history of furniture is of use to you the reader to enable appreciation of the possibility of finding yourself with a valuable piece of furniture on your hands. Should this be the case, do not charge merrily ahead and make repairs or modifications which could then damage the piece´s authenticity.

TABLE LEGS

From left to right and top to bottom:
Turned elements on flat faces (1600–1645)/ Turned in balustrade (1600–1645)/ Turned with melon bulb (1600–1645)/ Turned in inverted cup shape (1660–1700)/ Double volute (1600–1645)/ Turned with cord and rings (1660–1710)/ Cabriolet (1720–1770)/ Three levels of false columns (1750–1775)/ Carved Greek (1750–1775)/ Cabriolet (1750–1775)/ Tapered (1760–1790)/ Yet more stylised taper (1760–1790)/ Tapered (1770–1790)/ Corded inverted cone (1800–1810)/ Sabre leg (1810–1830)/ Ring–turned (1810–1830)/ Victorian style balustrade (1835–1880).

CHAIR LEGS

From left to right:
Double volute (1675)/ Volutes in opposing direction (1690)/ Combination of turned and carved (1660–1730)/ Turned wreathed column (1670–1700)/ Double–turned intertwined (1670–1700)/ Cabriolet ending in horse´s hoof (1715–1730)/ Cabriolet (1715)/ Cabriolet ending in clawed–ball (1755)/ Fluted tapered column (1760)/ Adam style (1775)/ Flute shaft with grooves (1775)/ Turned and fluted (1780–1790)/ Sheraton style with butt (1780–1800)/ Turned with taper and butt (1785)/ Turned, rings and butt (1780–1800)/ Sabre–shaped (1810)/ Sword–shaped (1790–1810)/ Cane decorated with facets (1810).

CHAIR BACKS

Turned sides and crosspieces (1680–1720)/ Wavy crosspieces (after 1720/ Shaped with turned sides (1720)/ Turned bars and sides (1750–1780)/ Chippendale with ribbons (1754)/ Chippendale Chinese inspired (1754)/ Studded leather (1775– 1800)/ Federal style, oval–shaped (1790–1800)/ Hepplewhite, shield–shaped (1794)/ Shield–shaped, Hepplewhite (1794)/ Hepplewhite, squared (1794)/ Sheraton, lyre– shaped (1802)/ Sheraton style (1802)/ Sheraton, entwined ribbons (1802)/ Sheraton, oval and central palm (1802)/ Sheraton, other variation (1802)/ Sheraton (1802)/ Sheraton, bars (1802)/ Sheraton, shield–shaped (1802)/ Other Sheraton design (1802)/ Sheraton, crossed bars (1800–1810)/ Sheraton, crossed bars and struts (1800–1810)/ Imitation Rococo (1850–1880)/ Imitation Renaissance (1860– 1900).

Rustic chest of drawers. One of the greatest satisfactions felt by a restorer is to find a piece of furniture which, when properly treated, recovers its solidness and appearance, making it one of the best pieces of a furniture collection. These pages will take you step-by-step through the transformation of a rustic chest of drawers found in a totally abandoned, thoroughly dirty state. The first step in restoring it consists of a careful examination. The whole piece of furniture is made from solid pinewood. The style is rustic and may well date from around the 20th century.

1/ A ruined piece of furniture in a deplorable state, seemingly impossible to restore it back to its original state.
2/ On the side, remains of paint, the wooden pieces seem to be really damaged by mould or dry rot, even the nails are well-rusted.
3/ If the frame is in bad condition, the drawers are in an even worse state: they drop down when opened, slats are missing out of the bottoms, many of the handles and fronts are broken and badly scratched.

4/ Nevertheless, the traditional workmanship can still be clearly seen on the piece of furniture. On the top drawer, for example, there is less bottom than on the other three and the lower part of the side forms the legs via an elegant curve.
5/ This photograph shows the really bad state of the wood used to form the structure and fronts of the drawers: splintered, chipped, dents, etc.
6/ The back part of the chest of drawers is also made using large vertical boards, but here it does seem to be in better condition that the rest of the piece of furniture (maybe because it hasn't been repeatedly painted or knocked about so much owing to it being up against the wall).
7/ Besides being rather badly mistreated, the wood of the legs is also cracked and broken.
8/ At some time or other, the top board was probably covered by marble. Hence it having a different appearance from the rest of the piece of furniture.
9/ View of the drawer's front and of one of the carved wooden pommels still left on this side.

Having checked the state of the piece of furniture - really damaged in this case, but at least it's free of woodworm holes - it's time to start work. The artisan who made this chest of drawers wasn't very knowledgeable as to cabinetmaking, he could well have been a shepherd who, because of the leisure time forced on him by winter, spent his time working the wood without having great machining resources to hand. He achieved a solid, handsome piece of furniture working from a simple plan.

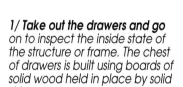

1/ Take out the drawers and go on to inspect the inside state of the structure or frame. The chest of drawers is built using boards of solid wood held in place by solid strips.

2/ When stripping, begin by taking out all of the drawers which will be dealt with separately thereby leaving the structure uncluttered and free for working on it.

3/ Choosing the right product for stripping is simplicity itself. Because this is an old piece of furniture, the best choice is to use Oxalic acid diluted in water (see pp 56 to 59).

4/ The drawers also have to treated individually, the painted parts in particular. This piece of furniture has been given several coats of paint aside from a primer coat of plaster with binder.

5/ Continue until all remains of the plaster have been removed (a process similar to that of Italian lacquering where several coats of plaster dissolved in binder are applied, rubbed

down between coats prior to applying the colouring coat).

6/ After carrying out the thorough cleaning implied by stripping, the drawers will look a whole lot better. The solid pinewood can now be appreciated.

7/ Once the piece of furniture is clean, check that the drawers work properly before going on to make the necessary repairs.

8/ Use a sponge or an artist's

brush to apply the stripper (according to where you have to reach), and rub vigorously with coarse aluminium wool (metal scouring pad).

9/ The piece of furniture's framework should also be stripped and rinsed off until it is fully clear of all remains of the stripper. Don't forget to take all the recommended precautions for using and handling toxic products.

RUSTIC CHEST OF DRAWERS

27

It is now when the real state of each one of the component parts of the chest of drawers can be seen, as well as that of the wood itself. The bottoms of the drawers *(some parts missing),* have to be rebuilt as well as some of the structure's joins needing repair. It has been oft-stated that the best course of action is to keep as much as possible of the piece of furniture original as possible, so only those parts missing will be replaced with new ones.

1/ In the photograph, how to fit the slats forming the bottom of the drawers is shown, and using a chisel, the projecting edges are cut down.

2/ To finish off the missing part, fit a piece of wood -pine- which will form the central bracing strip for the drawer's width. The slats are then fitted in the side grooves of the drawer and are lightly nailed on their ends.

3/ Fit the crosspiece strip by gently tapping on the ends of the bottom slats. This will now be complete and will be strong enough to support the weight.

4/ As could be seen when inspecting the piece of furniture, some of the bottom slats from the drawers were missing and have to be replaced.

5/ It is essential that the new wood parts are of the same type of wood (pine), same thickness and are properly seasoned so that the new wood doesn't cause movements which would cause damage to the original wood.

6/ The inside of the top drawer of the chest of drawers has lost the covering veneer and it has been decided to replace this with a nicely-grained veneer which will match the front of the chest of drawers.

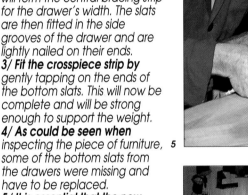

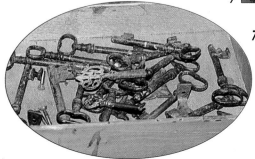

7/ This photograph shows the three complete drawers fully assembled. The differences in the bottoms is due to keeping the original parts as much as possible.

8/ View of the inside of the drawer with its lock and repaired bottom.

9/ The same drawer seen from underneath. The light nailing of the slats to the drawer's sides can be seen here, as well as the central crosspiece strip used to give support.

It would be easier to replace all of the handles for new ones, but this would greatly lower the worth of the piece of furniture. As would any other conscientious restorer, the one working on this piece prefers to do the work by hand using the original pieces remaining as models for the replacement parts. Making them in a lathe would be simplicity itself, but they can also be made artisanally on a carpenter's bench using handheld tools.

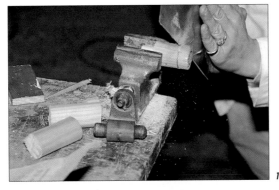

1/ Cut as many cylindrical pieces of the right size (totalling the length of the central and end parts) as there are handles missing.

2/ Firmly grip the piece in the carpenter's vise, mark out the circumference needed as a guide (this will be the diameter) in order to cut the end ball.

3/ Cut down with a chisel. First, give it a cylindrical shape smaller than the central part.

4/ If all of the handles are cut and each stage done at the same time, this will make the job that much easier and they will all turn out the same.

5/ Use a rough file to give shape to the rounded form which will first be cylindrical and then a half sphere.

6/ Continue working with the edge of the file to get the required shape and round off the end. Smooth down.

Before going on to varnish, apply a light water dye with aniline to the bare wood. On the pages dealing with transparent finishes, a section is given over to rubber lacquer finishes (p 71). This is a special product; it is a resinous substance which has a great affinity for wood, thereby protecting it and making it more alive. It can be bought ready for use or, better yet, you can make it yourself.

7/ The proportions are: 225 g of rubber lacquer in flakes, 7 g of benzoin and 15 g of sandarac in a litre of denaturalised high- grade alcohol.

8/ Mix all the ingredients together in a glass jar (coloured glass), and shake well before use.

9/ A more dilute solution can be used for the first coats (applied with a brush), though as we are dealing with old wood here, a special primer is not really needed.

This resinous substance, sold in flake form, comes from the exudation from some trees (*some types of Ficus, Croton, Ziziphus and Mimosa*), when they are bitten by the pregnant female of the Coccus lacca, together with the remains of the insect itself. In the manual (*p 71*), the method of preparing the pads and suchlike implements for applying the lacquer is described, recommendation is made to first impregnate some of them and keep them in a sealed container thereby making them easier to use.

1/ *Coloured or white fabric can be used. These, however, must always be cotton so that they don't leave fluff behind which could stick to the wood which is being finished.*

2/ *This is the proper way of holding the pad, ensuring that the part which comes into contact with the surface being varnished doesn't form a wrinkle which may leave a mark.*

3/ *Do not leave drips, splashes, use fast, firm strokes as fine as possible. Leave to dry between coats and then rub using fine aluminium wire wool prior to cleaning and applying the next coat of varnish.*

4/ *The powder produced by rubbing down is used as a kind of pore filler and gives the smooth surface characteristic of this finish.*

5/ *Polishing has to be done over all of the surface equally, including the edges and corners. This is then cleaned using a clean dry cotton cloth.*

6/ *It is essential that rubbing down be uniform and done in all directions so that the surface is left completely smooth.*
The amount of varnish powder produced by rubbing down is quite considerable.

7/ *For the second coat, repeat the process as per the first. It is best to apply a good number of coats. One of the most important conditions to ensure that varnishing turns out well is that each coat is thoroughly dry before the next one is applied.*

8/ *These photographs show the second coat of varnish being applied and you can now begin to appreciate the depth and intensity of the shine which characterises this type of lacquer.*

9/ *It must also be borne in mind that the lacquer has to be applied to all parts of the piece of furniture. If at all possible, it is advisable to apply varnish onto horizontal surfaces (turning the chest of drawers over to achieve this).*

With the shine and colour of the finish, the pinewood of this chest of drawers has taken on a magnificent appearance. It is still a rustic piece of furniture, but is now worthy of gracing the most select settings.

The signs of the passing years are still visible and, as is desirable in a good piece of restoration work, it is still an antique piece of furniture, which is now useful as well as being beautiful.

1/ The reproduction of the handle is the same as those already fitted and on the strip which separates the two drawers, a chip has been left thereby retaining some of the piece of furniture's rusticity.

2/ The lock, suitably cleaned, has regained the golden gleam of the original brass.
The colour and shine of the drawer's front and top are identical thanks to the painstaking varnishing of them.

3/ The simplicity of the joins between the wooden components has been retained (wood-wood and held in place by the interior strips).

4/ The bottoms of some drawers have been varnished but not in a like fashion, others have been left as they were originally. With the interior repairs carried out and the cleaning of the coats of paint, the drawers now work and are perfectly preserved.

5/ A good restorer isn't trying to hide repairs made, but is instead trying to keep and preserve as much of the original as possible. The back has been lightly dyed but, as is natural, not varnished.

6/ This frontal view shows the magnificent results obtained on this piece of furniture.

7/ The restoration even reaches the bottoms of the drawers just like all other parts of this chest of drawers. The front and sides of each drawer are assembled with half-hidden dovetail joins.

8/ The varnishing has enough shine and depth appropriate to

the chest of drawers's rusticity. On other pieces of furniture, the number of coats will be greater.

9/ It is interesting to turn back these pages and compare this photograph with the first ones

taken when studying the piece of furniture in its original state... All the time and effort put in can be safely said to have borne fruit indeed!

CLASSIFICATION OF JOINS. These joins unite pieces of wood together and don't need any kind of nails or screws, thereby making a more natural union *(one where both parts hold the other and allow inherent expansions and contractions of the materials)*. They can also be glued and offer great, long-lasting service for years on end. There are a lot of join types thanks to the multiple combinations created by good cabinetmakers. There were epochs when the great furniture makers invented new joins which we so disguised under the subsequent finish, that it was almost impossible to distinguish the different pieces. A well–made join is an elegant, strong way to build furniture. A restorer has to have a certain knowledge of the different kinds in order to be able to carry out the necessary repairs *(gluing or ungluing, adding to deteriorated parts, etc.)*, in this classification, you can find the more commonly used joins with some complicated ones thrown in.

Flat joins.
1/ Loose tongue, joins two grooved planks and is used for tabletops, panels, etc.
2/ Tongue and groove, is the most commonly used one for making panels, tabletops, floors, etc. Generally sold ready for assembly.
3/ Half join, this join is used straight or on corners and is normally found on simple furniture.
4/ Dovetail joins. When used for boars, form solid, very strong joins. (It is the one recommended for joining boards which tend to crack).
5/ With this dovetail join, a board can be extended and the end result is very strong.

1

2

3

4

5

Joins for struts, beams, etc.
6/ Central mortise and tenon, done like this, it extends or repairs a beam.
7/ Also with a central mortise and tenon join, this join connecting two struts in a T. Used on a great many parts of pieces of furniture.
8/ This kind of join is called a waiting join and is used to strengthen a beam, the legs of a table, etc.

Joins making corners, right–angles generally.
9/ The half join is also used to form corners on simple pieces of furniture. Nails strengthen the join's solidity.
10/ A more elegant solution is the mitre join, the union is made stronger by using dowel pins.
11/ The half mortise and tenon join, keeps the side free of all hints of the join.

6

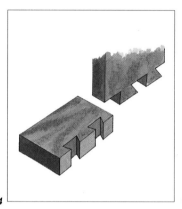

7

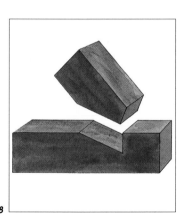

8

9

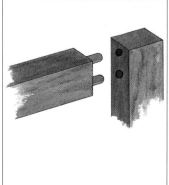

10

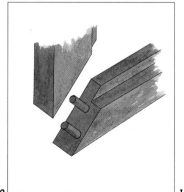

11

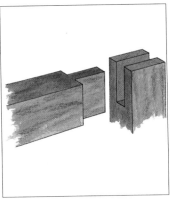

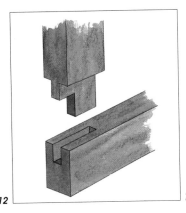

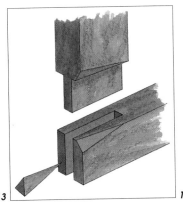

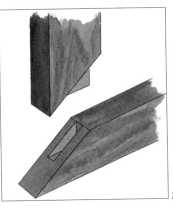

16/ The hidden mitred mortise and tenon join makes an elegant, strong solution for a cabinetmaker's corner.
17/ A mitre join is the typical union made on picture frames and mouldings. If glued only, it should only be used for lightweight constructions.
18/ False mitre join: on one side the typical diagonal line can be seen, on the other, the join is strengthened by a butt.

12/ Full mortise and tenon join, very solid but rather high profile.
13/ Half-heel mortise and tenon join, the heel's shape greatly strengthens this join which is used for form strong corners.
14/ Butt join, another variation of the mortise and tenon, but here with a wedge which disguises the true point of the union. Recommended for woods which will be veneered later on.
15/ An elegant, very solid solution for making corners: mitre join with hidden pins in dovetail.

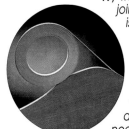

19/ The butt join with splayed mitre, is typically used for framing (glass, panels, etc., which is inserted in the groove).
20/ Hidden dovetail joins, typically used for the front of a well-made drawer.
21/ Double mortise and tenon join with base tongue, additionally strengthened with wedges and constituting a clear example of a complex join, but necessarily so in some cases.
22/ Another variation on corner or mitre joins, here strengthened by a pin in the corner.
23/ A loose tongue can also be used to strengthen the mitred corner join.
24/ This time, an elegant solution, the loose tongue of the mitre join is hidden.
25/ Another combination of mortise and tenon with mitre appearing on one side.

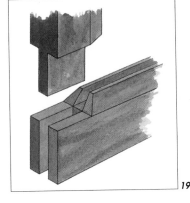

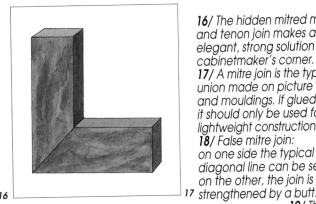

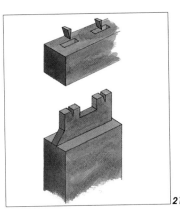

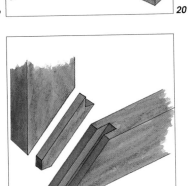

TREATMENT FOR BURNS. This process is aimed at restoring solid woods or superficial burns on veneers given that when the burn goes beyond the veneer, it will be necessary, to also replace the corresponding layer of wood with a patch *(p. 50)*. Deep burns need careful handling. First, rub down the affected area with sandpaper wrapped around a section of rod *(3 mm thick roughly)*, or make it into a roll ending in a point with the same sandpaper.

1

2

5

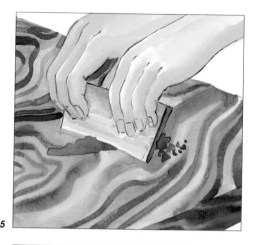

6

until reaching the desired hue.
Sometimes, two dyes must be mixed to get the right tone matching the original finish. Once melted and dissolved, pour into a clean empty bottle allowing it to solidify.
5/ Once hard, take from the container using a spatula and use your fingertips to soften up the filler.
Heat the blade of a putty knife over a flame, and put the wax on it allowing it to

3

4

1/ When rubbing down the blackened area, take care that the surrounding area is not rubbed down or this will remove the patina and make it more difficult later on to apply an even coat when giving the final varnishing.
2/ Once the carbonised wood has removed, should a toast colour be left behind, put a drop of whitener on a cotton cloth and rub until the desired tone is achieved. Rinse off and dry before continuing.
3/ The small marks left by the burn, once cleaned up, can be filled using wood filler, similar to a wax pencil.
Simply apply along the mark. When the mark is deeper, melt some drops off the bar and drip onto a previously heated putty knife. Spread out over the area to be treated, removing the excess by rubbing over with a cotton cloth.
4/ If the burn is deeper, it is advisable to make the filler yourself using beeswax and colouring: use between 60 to 125 g of beeswax and a vegetable or wood colouring (taking care that it is acid–based to ensure proper mixing with the beeswax). To make this filler, melt the wax in a bain Marie and add small amounts of colouring

melt and drip onto the damaged area until the mark is overfilled (take into account the wax's contraction on cooling).
Leave until the wax is fully hard and then carefully rub down and remove the excess using a safety razor. Rub vigorously to polish the surface.
6/ When the burn has been caused on a surface finished using rubber lacquer, follow the first three steps and then fill the burn mark with layers of rubber lacquer until reaching the level of the surrounding area.
Varnish over until all the edges are well-mixed by applying sparingly with a clean pad and repetitive movements in elongated eights.

Pressure must be kept light when applying to ensure that each pass leaves a fine film of varnish.
Examine your work from time to time to ensure that the result is uniform and allowing sufficient time for each coat to dry, this will give a better idea of
the effect. Leave the last coat to dry for 24 hours and apply the finishing touch: using a new, clean pad soaked in denaturalised alcohol, go over the surface very lightly and quickly, using first a figure of eight movement and then from fore to aft (in the direction of the woodgrain), applying more pressure with the pad.
This procedure will give the finish that desirable high sheen and the burn will have thus been vanquished.

SCRATCHES AND MARKS. All marks which happen on furniture have to be repaired as quickly as possible, this will make it easier to get rid of them. At all events, always try to use a simple method first before going on to another more energetic one. For example, when the mark has happened without breaking the wood fibres but has left a dent in the wood's surface as a result of a knock or excessive pressure brought to bear *(called indentation)*, the best system to try first is the one detailed below.

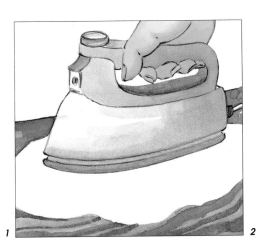

1

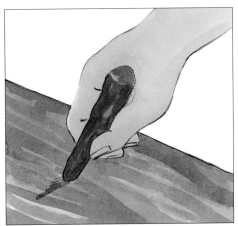

3

4

1/ Fill the dent with hot water, this make the compressed fibres swell up and dilate, returning them to their original volume and filling the dent.
If this is not enough, put a wet cotton cloth on the indentation and heat it up using an electric iron hot enough to produce steam. Take care to limit the contact of the iron to the damaged area alone.
Use the tip of the iron when the dent's extension is small, and the whole base of the iron when dealing with a larger area. Prior to continuing with the repair, leave the affected area to dry completely. If the wood has been dented to such an extent that it is not possible to bring it back to its previous normal level, recourse must be made to the same treatment used to fill scratches, cuts or scoring which have caused broken fibres.
2/ When the scratch or scoring is slight, these can be filled by applying bar lacquer (also called bar filler, wood putty or cabinetmaker's wax), which you can buy in the same colour, or one as close a match as possible, as the wood you are repairing.
It looks like a thick pencil and is applied in a likewise fashion: by "drawing" over the line of the mark.
3/ If the mark is deeper, melt a little of the bar (heating it over a match so that it drips onto the blade of a heated putty knife). Spread out over the area to be treated. This filler hardens fast, when cold, rub over with a cotton cloth to remove any excess. If the exact colour match can't be found, you can make the filler yourself using beeswax and colouring as explained on the previous page.
4/ When repairing a series of splinters, holes, cracks, scratches or the wood itself has an extensive area of dilated pores, use proper wood putty filler to fill these defects (a fine sawdust base mixed with carpenter's glue until a homogenous paste is formed).
This mixture can also be found in DIY stores and hardware shops and you only need to

add the water required (follow the maker's instructions). This filling paste is then applied using a putty spatula.
It must project out well above the level of the surrounding surface because when it dries, it tends to contract quite a lot.
If it has dried leaving a rough surface, rub or polish this down to leave a smooth surface.
If the colour of the mixture is too light, add a little sienna or dark earth pigment. It is highly important to exactly match the filler's colour with the surrounding wood when the finish used is transparent varnish.
5/ When the finish of the surface has to be painted, simply prepare the filler with one part calcium carbonate to three parts plaster of Paris.
Tint with a powder pigment (if the colour isn't too dark, it may not even be necessary).
Add enough water to form a paste and apply with a trowel or spatula, as per the previous step.

5

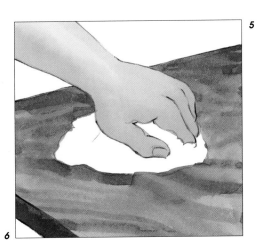

2

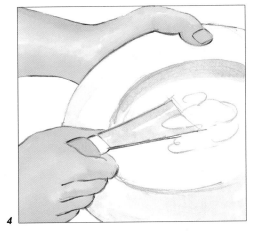

6

6/ The white points or circles which form on wood owing to moisture from glasses or hot plates can be repaired by rubbing the stain with a clean cotton cloth, previously moistened with camphorated alcohol.
You can also use a solution made of half-and-half turpentine (or ammonia) and linseed oil. You can also use the polish used to clean brass.

WOODWORM. Woodworm could be classed as the worst enemy of antique furniture. When buying a piece of furniture, particularly if it is old or simply secondhand, minutely inspect each and every part with great care. Should one single wooden piece be infected by woodworm, it could mean that all furniture in the vicinity of the affected piece will end up being infected too within relatively few years. Woodworm is a flying beetle *(hence its ease of movement from one place to another)*, but the dangerous phase of its life cycle is when it is in the larval stage. It can and will attack all kinds of furniture and almost all kinds of wood but will generally install itself in the undersides or rears of wardrobes, chest of drawers or drawers which have not been varnished or which are normally made of softer woods.

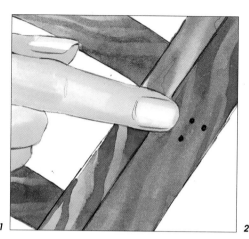

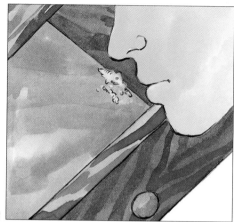

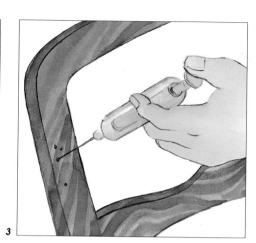

1/ Woodworm generally begins its work because it has been introduced into the home inside a piece of wood or plant shoot infected by it. The insects emerge in July or August and fly off to deposit their eggs thus infecting other pieces of furniture.
The outward mark they leave on the surface may be as small as the head of a pin but inside, the galleries can be very long indeed and run to all corners weakening the piece, leading to the eventual breakage of any of the infected parts.

2/ When inspecting a piece of furniture, look for small piles of sawdust on the floor immediately underneath the piece or inside it. Be doubly suspicious if any rear or underside sections have been recently replaced, it could be that the woodworm has irreparably damaged these parts necessitating their replacement.
It is, however, a sure bet that it will have attacked other, less visible parts too. The inside of recent holes is fresh and light coloured, the older ones darkening with time. The piece of furniture must be treated as soon as possible to stop the infection spreading further as this will undermine its structural integrity.
When the wood is pressed using the blunt side of a knife blade and this gives without offering resistance (or breaks, even), this means that the piece is seriously damaged.

3/ Some parts of the piece of furniture can be replaced, but the rest will have to be treated. The first step consists of isolating the piece in a garage or workshop thereby impeding the woodworm spreading to other pieces of furniture. Next, treat it using a commercial anti-woodworm solution, petrol or paraffin oil followed by wood alcohol or liquid ammonia. To apply the product, each hole must be injected with it using a pointed nozzle (a large syringe or clean oilcan can be used for this).

4/ Each hole has to be injected with enough liquid to ensure the larva is reached by it.

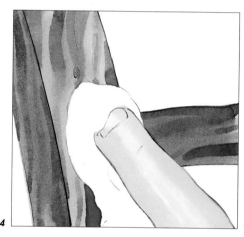

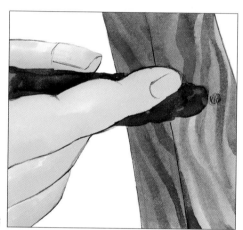

Whenever possible, work from the back or interior so as not to damage the piece's exterior. After waiting 24 hours, wipe of the excess which has oozed out.
Keep the piece isolated and keep watch to be sure that the infection has been eradicated. Applying anti-woodworm treatment with a brush on the unvarnished parts of the piece of furniture is always a good idea.

5/ To hid the holes left: fill using a cabinetmaker's wax bar of a matching colour (as per the instructions for filling any other kind of hole given on p. 35).
If a wooden part has been severely weakened, such as the end of a leg, turn the piece upside down and wrap the affected part with cardboard forming a sleeve which extends beyond the area for some centimetres. Bind tightly around the outside using insulating tape and fill with a hot anti-fungicide glue solution which will penetrate all the woodworm holes.

6/ The glue will be dry after 24 hours and will have strengthened the affected wood.
If traces of glue or cardboard are left behind, rub down gently and apply varnish to level the area off. Whenever carrying out

a repair or renovating the varnish of a piece of furniture, it is advisable to take advantage of the occasion and apply a coat of liquid insecticide specifically for woodworm.
When this is dry, any kind of finish or varnish can then be applied. There are also varnishes and polishes which have insecticides incorporated and help to keep a permanent protective barrier in place.

ROT. It is highly unlikely that furniture used in a lived in home is affected by an excess of humidity to such an extent that the wood actually rots or mould, etc., appears.
This is not the case, however, in tropical countries where the temperature and humidity are high.
This may also be the case for pieces of furniture which have been in storage for a long term, stored under bad conditions or kept in uninhabited buildings.
The natural lifespan of wood varies greatly depending on the tree species it belongs to.

Perishable woods (less than 5 years out of doors): *birch, beech and balsa.*
Somewhat more resistant but not long-lasting (5–10 years): *pine, spruce, sequoia, poplar, lime, obeche and American red oak.*
Moderately durable (10–15 years): *Oregon pine, sapele and African mahogany.*
Long-lasting (15–25 years): *European oak, white American oak, mahogany from Brazil, meranti and red cedar.*
Very long-lasting (more than 25 years) *and therefore the best for outdoor use: teak, Guiana laurel, African teak and cherry mahogany.*
Obviously, when dealing with pieces of *furniture kept and used in homes, under*

The only care which must be taken of a piece of furniture affected by rot, consists of replacing the irreparably destroyed parts and treatment of the surrounding area, spraying it and its surrounds with a commercial fungicide, as well as ensuring it is located in the right conditions. Infected wood feels powdery to the touch and has a musty smell. A very effective way of applying the fungicide –though not always possible– is to impregnate the piece (using a pressure based system in a vacuum chamber).

normally ventilated conditions at non–excessive temperatures and humidity levels, these can be kept in perfect conditions for a great deal longer whatever their wood type.
Nevertheless, if wishing to move an antique piece of furniture to a tropical climate, special care must be taken to ensure that it is properly preserved and does not literally disappear in the space of a few short years under a layer of mould and fungi.
These data are of particular importance when dealing with woods used in building, for floors and garden or terrace furniture, however, when dealing with the conservation, restoration or repair of antique furniture they are merely to be used as a guide.

STAINS. The best way of getting rid of any stain on wood furniture is to clean it off as quickly as possible. If it hasn't penetrated into the wood, only the shine of the surface will have to be rectified. Sometimes, simply rubbing over with a cloth after mopping up the spilt liquid is enough. However, on other occasions, when the spillage has gone unnoticed until it is too late and has seriously damaged the varnish or penetrated right into the wood's fibres, it then becomes necessary to use a more in-depth repair process. Each stain type may need a different treatment, thus, the first step is to ascertain with the greatest accuracy what caused the stain thereby ensuring you apply the right treatment.

On some pieces of furniture, it is not a case of removing determined stains, but is instead a general cleaning or of giving new life to a damaged coat of varnish.

1/ Oil or grease stains disappear using benzine or petrol. The problem is that these products affect the veneer's varnish or adhesive. It is better, therefore, to first try spreading a thick layer of talcum powder over the stain, covering it with several layers of white tissue paper and gently heating it with an iron (set to wool temperature and NO steam).
The talcum powder and tissue paper will absorb the grease or oil. This process can be repeated as oft needed until the stain has been completely removed.

2/ Alcohol, perfumes or medicines generally leave a white stain on varnished or rubber lacquer surfaces.
The only solution possible is to reapply the finish again (p. 70).
When dealing with synthetic varnishes, these are more resistant, the downside being that once damaged, the solution is more difficult because they are usually soluble in alcohol.
You can try rubbing down the exact area of the stain with very fine sandpaper which can then be subsequently delicately touched up with varnish.

3/ Wine or fruit stains, very rarely penetrate deeply into the wood. These can be cleaned up by gently rubbing down.
Then, using cotton wool, gently rub with a little hydrochloric acid followed by a few drops of hydrogen peroxide.
This method is also very efficient for old red ink stains.

4/ Blood can be removed with normal, everyday hydrogen peroxide or with a 5% solution of sodium thiosulphate, applied by gently rubbing on with cotton wool bud or cotton cloth.
It is better to proceed with caution, working first on a small part of the stain and then working further afield on it, changing the

cotton bud or using a clean part of the cloth.

5/ For ink stains, it is almost impossible to get it right first time; you'll have to keep trying different products until the right one is found.

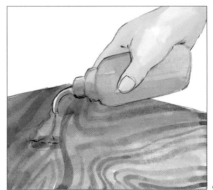

When the stain is recent, wash with water and then apply lemon juice with an absorbent cotton cloth to whiten it (you can also use cotton wool or a brush).
It is highly likely, however, that the stained area becomes damaged by the water and will have to be subsequently treated (see p. 35).

6/ When the ink stain is old, it is better to lightly rub down the stained area to remove the stain or until the wood is left bare. Cut off a piece of cotton wool the same size and shape as the stained area and pour on a little sulphuric acid, enough to just moisten the cotton wool, NOT leave it dripping wet. After leaving it on for two or three minutes, carefully check visually and if necessary, repeat the operation.
Another possibility consists of using oxalic acid diluted in hot water. This product also works for removing red ink stains.
When simply cleaning off general dirt accumulated on a piece of furniture over the years, caused by dust and lack of care, remember that removing the original finish of an antique piece of furniture could mean its losing part of its value.
For furniture which is not antique, before deciding whether completely removing the finish and reapplying it is necessary, try giving it a good cleaning using the following formula made in a bain Marie: one part turpentine resin to one of linseed oil (cooked). Soak a fine steel wool scouring pad and rub down the entire piece of furniture following the woodgrain. Leave for 15 to 30 minutes so that it penetrates and then clean off with a clean cloth.
As these are inflammable products, it is more prudent to first heat the water and then, with the recipient removed from the heat source, put the pot containing the ingredients in so that they amalgamate with the heat.

RESTORING HINGES. Fitted to wardrobes *(used for clothing or otherwise)*, tables *(leaf)* and doors alike, hinges can very often be the cause of problems when not working properly. They can stop the leaves on tables from coming up perfectly flush with the main table top, leaving them at an angle off horizontal. Doors of wardrobes or rooms can be stick when opening and closing or not close fully. Hinges don't only wear out over time and use, improper installation could be behind them not working properly. Very often, it is simply a matter of the screws having loosened up a bit, this is easily resolved by re–tightening them with a screwdriver of the appropriate size and type. To do this, simply tighten or loosen the screws gradually: a few turns for each one, until they are all tightened equally while supporting the door so that its weight does not come to bear on the hinge until this is properly fitted *(the bottom edge can be rested on something to support its weight).*

1/ If the holes in the wood have become enlarged or the surrounding wood is damaged or splintered: remove the hinge (in many cases, it will not be necessary to remove it entirely, only on the loose side will be enough). Then, fill the cracks and splinters with wood filler (or a mixture prepared using wood glue and sawdust until a consistent paste is formed) and leave to dry.

2/ Another solution for holes which are too large could be to fill them with small strips of wood (matchsticks coated with glue, for example), and when fully dry, proceed to fit the screws as fitted before. When the hole is large but not big enough to accept the strip

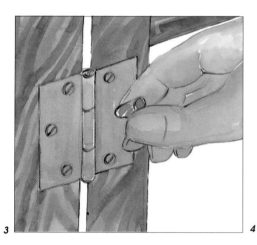

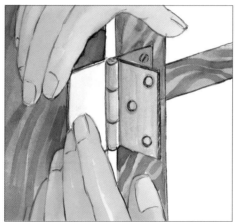

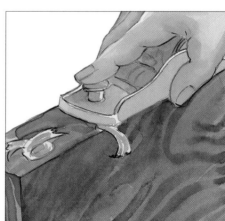

of wood we want to put in it, use a drill to make the hole large enough and then glue it in.

3/ A dowel pin can also be used. After insertion, cut of the protruding section with a chisel, and redo the holes using an appropriately sized drill bit.

4/ Sometimes the problem is that the hinge has been fitted too deep (the wood has been cut too deep for the hinge's seating). In this case, the simplest thing to do is to remove the hinge with a screwdriver, trace its outline exactly on a piece of thick cardboard, cut this out and then refit the hinge with the cardboard cutout between it and the wood mounting, then refit the screws.

5/ When the door doesn't

fully close, check to see that the hinge's mounting screws are not themselves sticking out too far and thus stopping the door from closing properly.

If tightening them up doesn't cure the problem, the next step is to remove the hinge and slightly deepen the undercutting (do this carefully, taking care not to overdo it as this could cause the problem covered in the previous point).

6/ In some cases where the wood has swollen owing to humidity (and if the problem doesn't go away when it is completely dry), the only solution possible to ensure that the door closes properly is to remove it and shave it down with a

carpenter's plane, on either the top, bottom or side where the hinges are fitted. Always take care to only take off enough to avoid the sticking point, but without overdoing it.

RESTORING DRAWERS. When a drawer sticks on opening or closing it owing to moisture, the best answer is to wait until atmospheric humidity drops, it dries out and then apply a coating of wax (*or soap*) on the sliding surfaces, this will ensure that it doesn't absorb so much moisture in the future. However, when this remedy fails, other solutions will have to be resorted to. If the wood doesn't return to its original state, it can be rubbed down a little on the drawer's side using rough sandpaper and always going with the flow of the woodgrain. Another cause of drawers not working properly, particularly in those pieces of furniture which have been repainted several times, could be that dried paint drops are large enough to make the runners stick. These can be removed with a scraper and solvent. If this still does not remove the problem, more drastic measures may have to be resorted to.

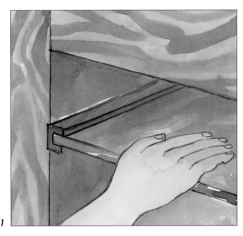

1/ There are pieces of furniture which have a board between each drawer fixed in place immediately underneath the runners. If this is warped or broken, it could stop the drawer from sliding. The best option here is to replace it with a new one.

2/ Generally, almost all drawers have their corners formed by the front (of better quality wood), the sides and the back wall, joined by dovetail joints.

The back wall is usually made of thinner section wood and is held in place by being slid into a groove on each side expressly there for this purpose, prior to joining the back wall with the rest.

3/ If the joints have become loose, it may be necessary to dismantle the drawer and then reassemble it and gluing the joints again, thereby ensuring that each join forms a right angle and the whole unit is properly rectangular in shape, using clamps or presses to hold it firmly.

When one of the pieces forming the drawer is broken beyond repair, the simplest step is to replace it using a wood matching the original as closely as possible.

When it is the front piece which is damaged, a patch can be applied which replaces the damaged part, great care being taken to match and reproduce the mouldings and blend the new part in with the old as seamlessly as possible.

4/ Sometimes, possible causes of a drawer sticking are worn or broken guides.

On the sides of the drawer, saw off the worn or irregular part and stick a new strip on. When this is fully dried, smooth off with sandpaper.

When it is the guide itself which is broken, it is best to replace it with a new one which can be glued or nailed in place in the corresponding groove.

There are several systems of guides depending on the size of the drawer and the furniture type.

If one of the joins on the drawer's side or back is broken, repairing it using a patch to rebuild it may be a delicate and ultimately unsound solution.

On the majority of pieces of furniture, this part is made using simpler wood and does not have the same importance given to more visible parts of the piece, thus, the

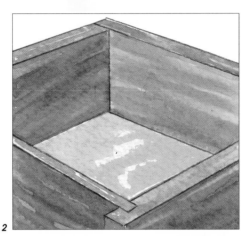

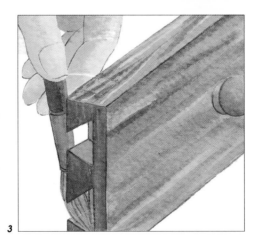

best solution here is to replace the entire side (or the broken piece itself, providing it is not the drawer's front).

Choose the right wood, place it over the broken piece, the side for example, and mark out the exact size and outline along which the wood has to be cut.

Saw leaving sufficient margin for chiselling out the dovetail join.

Draw the notches (in the appropriate place) to ensure correct mating up with the adjacent piece and then cut them out. This job can be slow and quite delicate using a chisel, but is made greatly easier and faster if a router is used as well as giving

better results.

Using this tool and the proper bits, a great many cuts of different shapes can be made: rounding off edges, making grooves, mouldings, undercutting, fluting, etc., all depending on the shape of the bit used. The bit for making dovetail joins is used to make the joins traditionally used for making all drawers in properly made cabinetmaker furniture.

Obviously, the bit used for the notches on the replacement for the broken side must be of the right shape and size, matching those of the part being replaced.

When working with this tool, it is better to practise first on piece of wood to find the right speed of movement; if you push too hard when working, the motor speed drops and splinters the wood. If, on the other hand, you go too slow the wood tends to burn.

When the bit turns in a clockwise direction, this causes the apparatus to slightly deviate to the left.

The more powerful the motor, the easier it is to work with the router (a power rating of at least 1 HP is recommended).

The details to bear in mind, aside from the power rating, are aimed at increasing safety and are: an on/off switch within easy reach, a transparent plastic cover to give protection against splinters flying out from the cut, and a built in light which enables you to see clearly what you are doing. Also recommended are gloves, protective eye wear, etc.

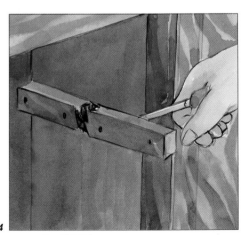

REPAIRING UNEVEN LEGS. All kinds of furniture fitted with legs can become wobbly at one time or another. The first thing to check is that it is in fact the legs which are uneven and not the surface it is resting on. To best way to do this is to put it on a known flat surface and see if it still wobbles. For ordinary pieces of furniture which do not have great value or age, the simplest solution is to even up the legs to match the length of the shortest one.

1/ Put bits of thin cardboard under the shortest leg until perfect stability is achieved.
The resulting total thickness of cardboard used will give the amount you have to cut off the other legs.
Use the cardboard's thickness to mark off each one of the other legs and then cut to the mark using a fine toothed saw.
The cut must be horizontal, irrespective of whether the legs are straight or angled.
Smooth the cut using sandpaper

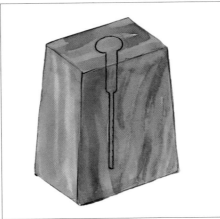

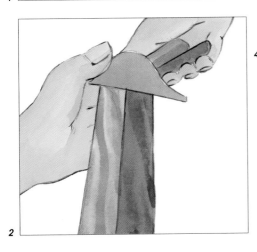

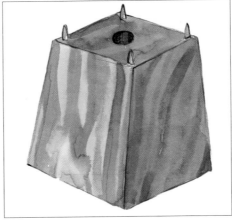

Select the right wood and cut it a little oversize to requirements.
Hold it in place and turn until deciding upon the best position for aligning the woodgrain for best possible alignment.
Mark this position and smooth the cut until fitting perfectly.
3/ Remove the butt and drill it with a drill to enable a long nail to be introduced in the join. Then countersink the hole's upper part to enable the nail head to be covered with a dowel pin.
4/ To ensure that the butt stays perfectly aligned with the leg, use four, 2.5 cm long nails, one on each corner.
Cut off the heads of the nails 0.5 cm from the surface and gently hammer them in until they just hold the butt in place.
5/ In this position, put a bit into the holes previously made in the butt, extend into the leg until they are the same length as the previously introduced nail.
Remove the butt to enable all sawdust or dust to be removed from the surface and hole.
Apply glue and refit in the previous position.
Drive the nail fully home now.

To cover the hole in, glue and fit a dowel pin in the part countersunk expressly for this purpose.
6/ When the glue has fully set, put an adhesive strip on the edge situated above the butt. This protective measure will avoid the wood being damaged when resting the fine hand saw which is to be used to cut off the excess wood.
Polish and finish off using a little pore sealant on the join's gap, match up the colour and

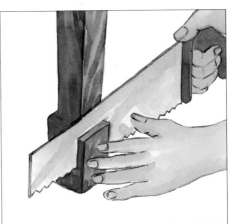

and rectify the finish if necessary.
2/ This treatment is not recommendable for antiques or quality pieces of furniture given that even the smallest piece removed will immediately reduce its overall value.
In these cases, the solution is to add the part lost back on to the shortest leg.
When the length to be put back on is less than 5 cm, a butt can be fitted: use a saw to remove the minimum amount of wood necessary, leaving the cut as flat as possible. Carefully measure the length and width of the butt required for the rectification.

finish. In other cases, the add on could be differently shaped: diagonal, angled, etc., always taking care that the part added on is fixed as strongly as possible while as little as possible is removed from the original wood in the process.

REPAIRING BROKEN OR LOST STRUTS OR BARS. Of particular relevance on Windsor style chairs with their innumerable struts and bars, they being particularly susceptible to breakage, also on other kinds of chairs where breakage occurs of the back, casings, etc. These parts must be repaired as soon as possible before this damage gives rise to other, possibly more serious, breakages or the loss of the part broken off.

1/ In the event of breakage, glue the two broken ends together using the appropriate wood adhesive. Firmly clamp them in place while drying and leave to dry fully before rubbing down the excess adhesive.
To make the join stronger, one or two dowel pins can be used (mark the place with a nail, cut the head off to mark the place which corresponds on the other part of the broken piece, drill and fit the glue-coated dowel pin), clamp, etc.

2/ When having to replace a complete bar or strut, remove all remains of the previous part which may have been left in the hole, drilling them out with a bit if impossible to remove by any other method.

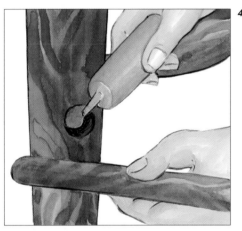

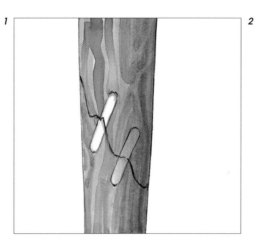

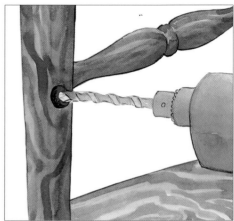

If dealing with a round-section bar, us a rod of the same diameter and calculate the overall length taking care to include those centimetres required for insertion into the chair ar back's upper section.
When the bar or strut is square or rectangular section, it may be necessary to glue together several strips until the right thickness is achieved.
If the piece of furniture is valuable, it will be best to get hold of a piece of the same type of wood and cut or turn it down to the right shape.

3/ Re-drill the hole again, using a chisel if this has to be square.
The hole will be of slightly less section than the bar or strut to ensure

tight fit. Cut the bar to the right size (adding on the length required to be inserted).
Slightly taper the ends using]paper and put a drop of ellulose-based adhesive on. Do the same for the other end.

4/ The same procedure will be used when replacing the struts of the casings, etc. the most difficult task is to ensure that carved or turned parts are reproduced faithfully, particularly if not having access to the machinery or tools which facilitate this job, and having to do the job manually.

5/ Windsor style chairs and armchairs are usually made using relatively simple woods uch as beech and yew.

Selection of the wood to use is generally dependent on differing needs according to the piece is will be used for: curved parts (like single piece forming the back and arms) need a more flexible wood than the turned parts (legs, casings, the first bar on each side and the struts which, in different sizes, fill the space between back and arms).
It is not usual for an amateur restorer to have an industrial lathe to hand allowing a duplicate of the turned parts to be made, manually turning the required bar needing a great deal of work and practice, even if having a simple bench to give shape using cutting tools while turning the piece.
If working entirely on a manual basis, the simplest way to get a round-section bar is to start with a square-section bar and then plane it down to an octagonal section and so on until achieving the desired curvature.
A similar method is used to obtain a tapered section on the ends or the central part.
However, for more complex designs, it is preferable to have a workshop make the copy for you (having first removed one of the whole pieces for them to use as a model).

REPAIRING CHAIRS. Chairs are probably the pieces of furniture which are used the most. Their structure is generally light and several parts are glued or joined by assemblies which not only have to support considerable weights, but very often, be used inappropriately as support for the user when he or she stands on the seat. There are a series of small problems which often occur: uneven legs, joins coming unstuck, etc. which, if not put right, can give rise to other more significant ones *(cracking, breakages or a loose join causing others to come loose too)*. One of the most frequent is the one where joins made using pins become unstuck.

1

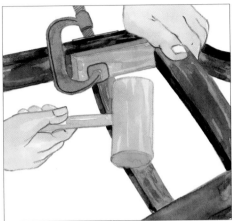

2

3

4

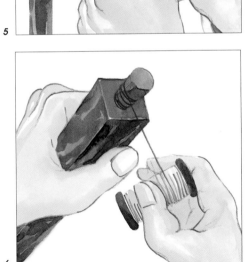

5

1/ When the rear legs of a chair extend to form the sides of the chair's back, something which very often occurs on chairs of the Biedermeier style. It is very easy for their join with the seat's frame to be stressed and work loose from the seat or the frame itself.

The most commonly used systems for these joins are chocks and dowel pins. They give the best results and appearance, screws which could be used for the same job tend to weaken the wood and are eyesores. This set up can be replaced without too much work and give splendid results. On the frame of the seat's lower section, on each corner, there are usually some triangular chocks to strengthen the join between the legs and the seat. If the chair is upholstered as shown in the illustration, remove the covering (or the backing and taping) to leave the pins fixing the seat exposed. Careful inspection of the chair will be necessary in each case to work out how to dismantle it properly.

2/ Remove the dowel pins, chocks or both. In some cases, it will be enough to gently tap them out with a wooden mallet or hammer (always put a piece of soft wood between the object and mallet or hammer to protect the chair from damage).

If they remain stuck in place, inject a suitable solvent over the join (drilling a small hole to enlarge the gap allowing the solvent to get in and work).

3/ The dowel pins holding the frame in place from the rear will also have to be replaced. If they

still remain stuck in place after using the previously given steps for the corner chocks, drill from behind or from inside the frame itself. Use a drill bit of the same size at the dowel pin, clean out the remains of glue left behind or of the pin.

It is advisable to wear eye protection against sawdust. Calculate the depth and put a strip of insulating tape as a marker on the drill bit so as not to drill too deep.

4/ Measure the depth of the holes with a pencil and cut the new dowel pins a little oversize. Gently tapping them almost fully home, marking off the projecting part at a distance of _ cm approximately.

Saw off at the mark using a fine-toothed saw. Remove the dowel pin, apply glue to the hole and evenly spread the coat using a toothpick.

5/ Fit the new dowel pin into the hole and drive fully home, gently tapping with a mallet or hammer. Immediately tighten the join firmly using clamps. Once dry, remove that part of the dowel pin which slightly protrudes using a chisel and, if necessary, make flush using fine sandpaper. Lastly, tint and varnish (or paint) if necessary to match

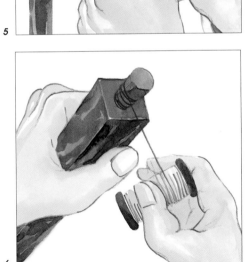

6

up with the rest of the chair.

6/ It could be the case that the dowel pin has come out but is still serviceable. A quick solution would be to wind a thread around it, glue being applied to both bound dowel pin and hole alike. Refit the dowel pin as previously described. Firmly clamp the join until the glue has set.

REPAIRING TABLES (with leaves). This page is given over to solving problems which commonly occur when restoring different kinds of extendible tables: extractable leaves, foldaway leaves, etc. (*to solve problems with legs, refer to p. 41, for the table's top, pp 47, 48 and the following ones for the repair of veneers*).
The first thing that generally has to be done is carefully inspect the hinges and their fitting: the fixing screws could be loose, etc. (*The advice given on p. 39 is applicable in that case*).

1/ On tables with drop down leaves, the first step is to open up the leaves and fit the supports in place. If the top "drops," does not stay horizontal (this can be verified with set square) or is not fully in contact with the support, the simplest way to correct this is to fit a wedge.
2/ The wedge must be at least the same length as the support and the requisite thickness to ensure that the top remains

sufficiently long–lasting, the wedge should be made of hardwood.
3/ If the table is used continually and has to bear frequent loads, it is better to fit a wedge longer than the support, one which reaches right to the edge of the tabletop. Fix in place with screws on the underside of the tabletop.
Obviously, if the leaf rests on two or more supports, all of these must be corrected until

lengthways beams difficult, you could also lightly wax them as per the steps detailed for drawer runners.
5/ In the case of some of the lengthways beams being broken or overly twisted to work properly, the best course of action would be to replace them for new ones.
6/ Remove the beam to be replaced, taking out the screws and cut another one of the same size and right shape (choose a

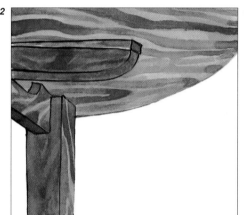

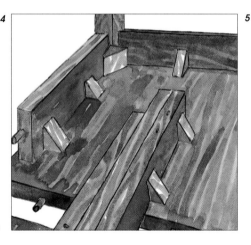

perfectly horizontal. If the wedge is only required on the end of the support, it can be fitted to the top across that end. To make the wedge

perfectly even support is achieved all–round.
4/ In the case of normal dining room tables with extractable leaves (which very often slide badly and are difficult to extract), it is necessary to remove the main tabletop altogether (this normally rests on two dowel pins and is easily lifted), and inspect the set of lengthways beams, check the screws (if these have become quite loose, it may be necessary to repair the holes: p. 39, step 1), or the glued chocks which are used as guides.
With the extensions fully open, carefully remove any dust and particles which may make the sliding of the

strong strip of wood of the same thickness and woodgrain). Both are then clamped in place to enable exact tracing of the end which tapers down and to then saw it carefully.
Fit the new strip with screws identical to the old ones.
When the edge of the leaf is lower than the tabletop, a piece of wood (glued in place) can be added, this should be of the thickness needed to leave the leaf level with the notch on the frame (as done when hanging a piece of furniture).

REPAIRING JOINS. There are a great number of systems for making the joins between different pieces of wood used to build so many diverse types and pieces of furniture. Basically, leaving aside those made using metal components such as screws, pins, etc., these can be reduced to a few kinds with multiple variations: butt-gluing joins, mortise and tenon, tongue and groove, bevel and dowel. This last type, in particular is used for several different ends: forming different angles, etc. Dovetail joins are also important (*typically used for making drawers*) and the combinations of different systems which are strengthened with pins. All of them can work loose or break with prolonged usage or by accident, but they can always be repaired by some careful workmanship.

1/ To repair pinned joins, the first step consists in cutting off the remains of the broken dowel pin flush with the wood it is inserted into.
Use a drill to eliminate any bits left inside the piece. A drill bit smaller than the dowel pin must always be used and do not go deeper than the original hole. If there are any bits left inside, extract them using a narrow chisel.
2/ Cut the new dowel pins from a rod of suitable diameter (can be purchased easily). Calculate the length of the new dowel pin (the depth of the two holes combined).
Taper the two ends slightly using a chisel, cut a notch in one of them with a saw as well as a V along the length of that part of the dowel pin which goes in to the holes to allow excess glue to come out.
3/ Thoroughly clean out both orifices (removing sawdust or old glue), and apply new glue, do the same on the ends of the dowel pin. Insert the dowel pin and press firmly home, holding it in place with a clamp or suitable pincer until the glue has set fully.

and inserted into the holes cut out on the spigot, tapping home with a mallet.
The end of the wedges may slightly protrude and when the glue has dried fully, cut off with a chisel. A dovetail join can also be repaired using the same method should it have become loose.
Another kind of join is the mitre join, this is widely used in framing (of pictures or

rectangular mirrors), and on the corners of mouldings. This join does tend to work loose or open up. If the problem is not too serious, simply filling the gap with wood filler prior to applying the finish should be remedy enough. However, when a significant breakage has occurred, it is better to replace the entire section and redo the corner.
Essential tools for making corner joins and for doing any work with mouldings and profiles are: pencil, fine hand saw (kept well-sharpened) or, better yet, an electrical saw specifically for mitre joins and a box for cutting mitre joins of good quality.
It is enough on a frame to cut the moulding at 45° with the flat side put up against the mitre box.
When dealing with fitting a frieze or skirting, however, interior corners will also have to be made as well as exterior ones.
For an exterior corner, offer up one of the parts to the wall and use a pencil to mark the outline of the frieze on the back of the adjacent skirting.
Cut the frieze following the outline marked

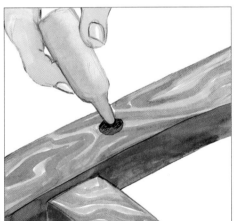

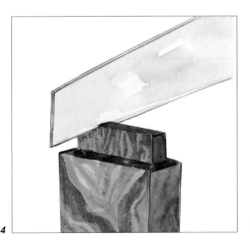

4/ On mortise (or tenon) joins, proceed in a similar fashion. In the case of breakage, remember that the spigot can be replaced just like a broken dowel pin: drilling out the hole (shaping it properly with a narrow chisel), then gluing a new spigot cut from strong wood to the right size and shape. If the join has merely worked loose, re-glue it (having first cleaned out any remains of the old glue).
5/ When, for whatever reason, the spigot has become too small for the housing, some bevelled notches on the end of the spigot can be cut (with a sharp chisel), and some hardwood wedges of slightly greater thickness. These are then glued as normal

(keep the bow saw perpendicular with respect to the skirting's face).
On fitting the two pieces, the frieze should line up on pressing it up against the skirting which forms the square.
The exterior corners are lined up with the two friezes cut at 45° with opposing mitres. To fit them, use headless nails which are embedded using a punch expressly for this purpose.

CHANGING PANES OF GLASS. Replacing broken panes of glass is one of those apparently simple jobs, but is in fact one which contains inherent difficulties, almost always occasioned as a result of lack of practice. One of the greatest problems is cutting the glass to the size needed. Technically, this is simplicity itself.

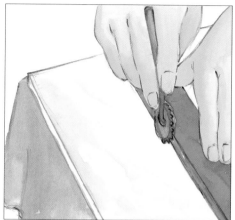

CHANGING PANES OF GLASS

46
.....

1/ Ensure the glass is well supported, laying flat on a surface covered by cloth and carefully cleaned.

2/ Use a ruler to trace a line with the diamond cutter (works better if the instrument's tip is moistened with a little light oil), trace said line with a firm hand (from the front and towards the person making the cut).

3/ Slightly raise the glass off the supporting surface and gently tap it underneath the cut made (encouraging the glass to break along the line traced).

4/ Wearing suitable gloves and with one thumb on each side of the line cut the glass in two using a small turn of the wrists.

It might be more practical, quicker and safer however, to take a piece of the broken glass to a glazier (so that you get the same size thickness and quality glass), and order the glass to be cut to size while there.

5/ The glass can be fixed to the piece of furniture or frame by means of putty, wood or metal strips (leaded glass). The fine wooden strips are held in place using fine nails: these can be removed with care and nailed back in again taking care not to touch the new glass.

6/ Metal strips are to be gradually opened using some fine pointed pliers. Once the glass has been fitted, re-close them taking care not to apply

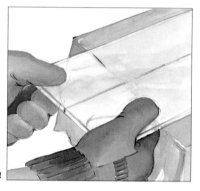

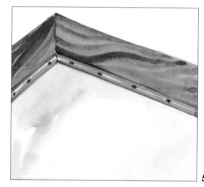

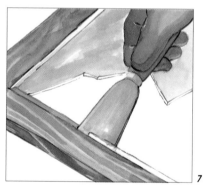

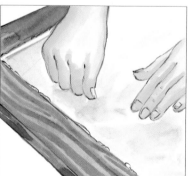

too much pressure (this can be made even more safer by using a putty with a colour similar to the metal's).

7/ When putty is used, the step by step procedure is: to carefully remove any shards of glass left behind together with any remains of the old putty –use gloves to do this. Soften the putty using a heat source.

8/ While the putty is being softened up, gradually raise it with a putty knife or glazier's knife. Knead the new putty on a sheet of newspaper (this may now be slightly tinted to match its colour to that of the putty holding the other glass in place). Mould the putty into a thin roll which is then pressed inside the moulding, advancing thus around the frame (put in a little at a time so that it is evenly distributed).

9/ Press the new pane of glass home (from the inside) up against the putty, ensuring that it is properly straight. Scrape off the excess putty from around the outside using a putty knife or scraper. Use another thin roll of putty to cover the interior forming a bevelled angle between the glass and frame. Ensure that the putty is not visible from the outside. Putty can be painted with a little oil paint to match its colour to the wood's.

REPAIRING WARPED WOOD. On the whole, the reason behind the warping of a board or one of the leaves of a tabletop, is that the upper part of the board has contracted while the underside has absorbed moisture from its surrounds *(ver often the dilation of the underside is due to the absence of finish on that part of the board with the subsequent ingress of moisture there).*

1/ The movement of the wood manages to remove the component parts holding it to the table or piece's framework. The solution here will depend on the thickness of the boards.
2/ If the board is more than 3 cm thick, it may be necessary to shape or so arrange the frame's lengthways beams so that the convex part of the top rests on the corresponding concavity.
3/ You can try to straighten out the whole top or each one of the boards which comprise the structure by wetting them and clamping them firmly flat using press clamps while they then dry out.

6/ Clamp the board flat up against a known flat surface until the glue has fully set. Then remove any excess glue, apply a finish and refit the tabletop onto the frame.

The absorptive capacity of wood for moisture is what makes it ideal for preserving books fabrics and so many other things normally held inside all kinds of wardrobes. These objects are protected from the abrupt impact of changes in temperature and humidity. It must be remembered that wood forming all parts of pieces of furniture is a "living" material which needs to contract and expand. The best, and longest lasting construction of a piece of furniture, is that which takes these characteristics of the material used into account. This movement is further accentuated by the thickness and dimensions of the boards used and also depends very much on how the wood has been "weathered."
Whether dealing with boards or panels held in place by a frame, they all need to have a certain freedom of movement, particularly when in contact with different kinds of wood, or with a fibre going in a different direction.

1

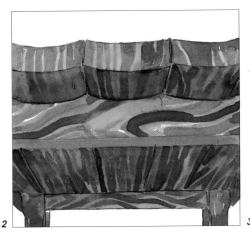

2

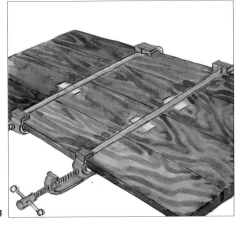

3

It will still be necessary, however, to strengthen the inside with strips of wood to stop further deformation. It is also advisable to apply the same finish to both top and bottom sections.
4/ When the tabletop is made of thick boards and these are greatly warped, it is best to remove them, mark the pieces (to refit them in the same order later on) and check that there are no nails or screws embedded in the wood.
Wet the concave side to help straighten this out.
As this remedy is merely a stopgap measure, when the boards are dry and flat, set the circular saw to cut to _ the depth of the board and then make cuts in each one of them at 2.5 cm intervals.
It is better to stop cutting before reaching the edges.
(These cuts release the internal stress on the board).
5/ When the boards have been grooved, glue thin strips of a similar wood inside each cut groove.

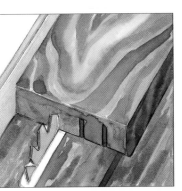

4

5

But, good quality wood, well- cut in regular boards which has been properly weathered and stored for the necessary time, will always have a certain movement, but it won't warp unless exposed to truly catastrophic conditions.
The piles of cut boards have to be dried placed on a flat base (normally some beams put on stone or brick), and properly levelled to ensure free circulation of air underneath it.
Grat care must be taken to ensure that all the wood is truly flat, any defect in its fitting will transmitted and affect the entire stack. This drying, done in the open, should take several months (each kind of wood needing a different length of time). The process is then continued in a closed warehouse using heating (better with warm air, a fan in the roof to force the air flow may also be used), which is kept at a constant temperature.

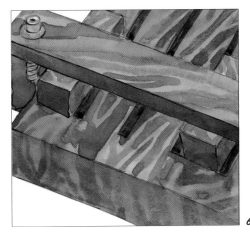

6

REPAIRING CRACKED WOOD. This problem generally occurs on wide parts *(comprised of several boards joined together)* on pieces of furniture made of solid wood. This is particularly the case when they have been moved from a place where the environment has been warm, to another with a high level of humidity. If the problem manifests itself on the joins of the boards, you can try to remove the affected pieces and refit them after having planed the edges of the joints. This system cannot be used when dealing with pieces with bracings or whenever it is not possible to change measurements.

1/ When a piece of wood cracks on its edges, it is impossible to repair it by gluing and pressing it back together. The best system is to insert a piece of veneer or thin strip of wood in the crack in the form of a wedge.

2/ The opening must first be prepared, making it even so that inserting the wedge is possible. To do this, it is best to first make the simple tools shown in the illustration: the blade is sharpened on both sides so that it can cut in both directions (both backwards and forwards). The cut width is controlled by the teeth both in front of and behind the blade (they being slightly misaligned in order to do this).

3/ The tool must be used following the direction marked by a ruler, resting the side and moving backwards and forwards until the crack is smoothed out and left as even as possible.

4/ Glue and insert the strip (when the repair is along the entire length of the board) or the wedge (when the crack only affects one end), ensuring that it is of a similar type wood and has the same woodgrain.

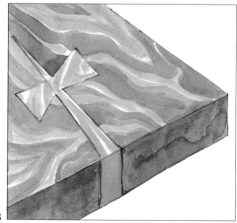

When this is dry, remove excess glue using a scraper, level the wood using chisel and smooth down with sandpaper.
This final work must be done on both the top and bottom sides.

5/ In some cases, when it is feared that the cracked wood will continue to open further, it is better to assure the repair by fitting a dovetailed tie on the other side, this acting as a bridge which will stop the wood cracking further open. It must be set in to a depth of roughly one third of the wood's thickness.
The edge of the tie must be slightly chamfered so that once fitted and glued in place, it will be held in place by pressure. The best answer to warped or cracked wood, is to use prime quality materials and proper construction techniques which take into account the inevitable and necessary

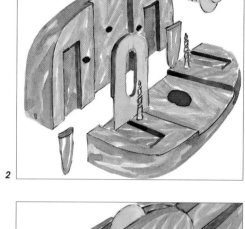

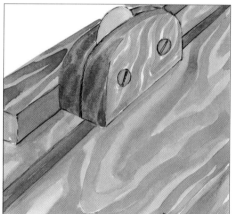

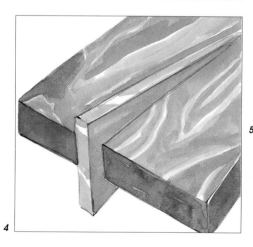

movement of a material which is not inert by any means.
Obviously, when dealing with a piece of antique furniture, the only course open is to try to repair the problems caused, very often, by the wrong construction process or faulty raw material.
One point which was common knowledge to furniture makers many centuries ago, is that for wardrobes, sideboards, etc., the rear of the piece of furniture is usually made of thinner wood than the other parts, it is not

glued nor held in place with nails: it is inserted into the grooves made for this purpose in the structure or the adjacent pieces. The whole structure, therefore, is endowed with the ability to expand or contract without reaching the point of breaking, cracking or warping.
The furniture maker's aim is not to ensure that the wood is used and becomes an inert material, but is instead to use it intelligently, taking advantage of its qualities and converting the problem into a challenge to the maker's skill.
Seeking to make the best use of a raw material which, though it be a renewable source, is being consumed at an rate which is outstripping the growth of forests, wood boards made of veneered plywood has been industrialised.
Thanks to the resins joining its components, this is a more inert material, more easy to work though never used for a quality piece of furniture.
Plywood is a highly versatile building material. It is made of thin layers or plies of wood which are laminated to form panels

of varying thickness and qualities, according to the ultimate need it is destined for.
When used for jobs requiring out-of-doors exposure, the plies are then treated accordingly.
Veneered plywood has an outer layer of fine grain wood, the other side being either the same or a common or garden wood variety.
Boards formed by strips, particles, etc., as is to be expected, are made with waste material: splinters, shavings or cheap woods.

REPAIRING VENEERS (dents, warped...)

1/ **when a stain has been left on the veneer,** but the backing wood has not been affected, this can be easily fixed: wet a cotton cloth with water, wring out and place over the wood affected.

Place a very hot iron on the cloth allowing it to produce abundant steam for a few seconds.

Do not hold the iron there too long as the rubber lacquer finish or under layer glue could be damaged as a result. Check to see that the stain has disappeared.

2/ **If the problem still persists, this will be** because the wood underneath has also been dented. The veneer will have to be cut over the mark and very carefully folded back, leaving the backing wood uncovered (carefully collect any fragment that may have broken off).

3/ **Use a spatula or stick if the area is very small** to fill in the dent in the base wood with wood filler. You'll have to put in enough filler so that it bulges out above the level owing to it shrinking when it dries.

When the filler is properly dry, lightly glue the back of the veneer and refit it.

Cover with cardboard and keep weighted down while it dries.

4/ **To fix the opposite type of problem, that is,** the veneer has warped (it has come unstuck from its base and a bubble has formed), this must be done in accord with the magnitude of the problem. Use a cork block to vigorously rub over the veneer (from front to rear following the grain). The heat generated by the friction may be enough to level out the blister without harming the finish.

5/ **If this system doesn't work, the next step is to** repeat it but this time rub using a hot iron (first protecting the veneer with a layer of cardboard). When the blister is soft, put and leave a heavy object on top of the cardboard for at least 24 hours to help make the veneer stick back in place.

6/ **If the veneer has not stuck properly, it will be** necessary to add a little glue on its underside. Use a well-sharpened blade (razor or cutter), cut the blister in the centre along the grain.

7/ **It may be that the wood under the blister is** dusty or powdery, this will have to be cleaned out using the tip of a brush.

When carrying out both this operation and gluing, press on one side of the blister (to work under the one that is raised), and then invert the working position to work on the other one. Press on both sides to squeeze out excess glue and clean this off with a moistened cloth.

8/ **If a cellulose-based wood glue has been** used, cover the glued part with white silk paper and leave to dry weighted down or clamped. If the glue is vinyl-based, pass a warm iron over the area and then leave there to cool down on the paper covering the veneer to help the glue to set.

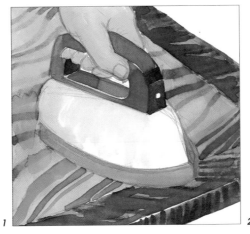

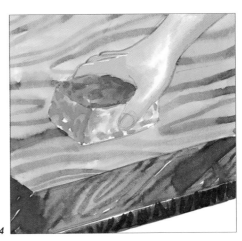

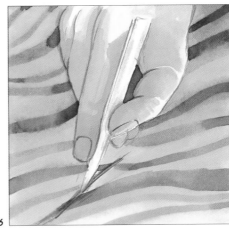

REPLACING VENEERS (parts). It is quite usual for a section of the veneer to come unstuck, particularly on the surface of a table or a drawer's front. If this problem is treated quickly *(re–gluing it)* it is simplicity itself to fix. However, if left for some time, it will eventually break off and the broken off piece of veneer becoming lost.

The first step then is to look for a piece of veneer matching the original as closely as possible: the same type of wood, grain and colour.

Nowadays, thanks to modern tools allowing a precise cut, veneers are much finer than before. This difference in thickness will in itself be another detail to resolve when obtaining a good result when restoring the piece of furniture.

1/ If the search for a veneer with the same thickness has been fruitless, cut a piece of tissue paper slightly smaller than the new piece of veneer replacing the old.
Leave to dry and then glue in place over the new piece of veneer.
If the difference in thickness is very noticeable, it may be necessary to glue two layers of veneer on or even a lamina of

splintered or split, it is better to give it a new regular edge for joining up with the new veneer. The general shape give to patches, whenever possible, is a rhomboid or oval (these are the shapes which allow better matching up of the veneer's grain and the rest of the surface).
Obviously, this will also depend on the siting of the patch: the edges, corners, curved

reverse side of the paper until it is dark gray. Place the paper with the penciled side upwards on the new piece of veneer and once again rub over the marked outline with the pencil. This can also be done on cardboard which can be used as a template for checking the exact match on the patch's site with the veneer.
6/ Carefully cut out the figure with an razor

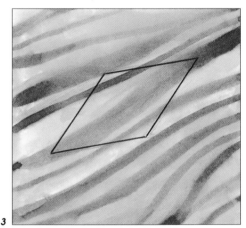

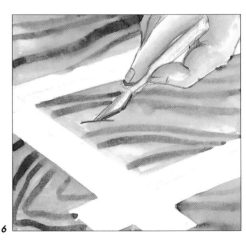

balsa wood.
2/ When it's the other way round: the new piece is thicker than the old one, you'll have to rub down the veneer prior to gluing it in place. A practical idea here is to make a ring of adhesive tape for fixing the veneer to the work bench, thus making it easier to rub down. When the piece is small, you'll have to wrap a thin strip of sandpaper around a wood block of suitable size, 4 x 4 x 4 cm, for example.
Rubbing down should always be done on the inside face and along the woodgrain.
3/ If the edge of the broken veneer has

surfaces, etc., also have to be adapted to other needs.
4/ In the event of repairing a corner on a flat surface: cut the edges using a blade to give it a regular shape. It's always better to have prepared a polygon of short faces than a square whose long sides will be more difficult to blend in.
To get the outline of the patch, trace this using tracing paper (transparent).
Using a sharp pencil is highly recommended as well as fixing the paper in place using adhesive tape, thereby ensuring that a clean, accurate tracing is made.
5/ Using a soft lead pencil, rub over the

blade or cutter, use a steel ruler. It is necessary to ensure a clean cut is made so that this coincides perfectly with the outline on the piece of furniture.
Carefully apply a cellulose–base wood or general purpose glue and clamp firmly with weights or clamps. It is always better to interleave a sheet of paper and wood to protect the veneer's surface.

7/ As a precaution, the new piece fitted can be left slightly overlapping the edges of the surface and, once the glue has dried, turn the piece around if possible and cut down with a very sharp blade from the back. The job can then be rubbed down lightly on the edges to blend it in with the original.

8/ Whatever the replacement patch be, particular attention must be paid to matching the patch as closely as possible to the veneer, that is, the same kind of grain, reflects light with a similar arc and the grain can be matched up on the edges.

9/ Sometimes, it isn't the veneer that has broken, but is instead a piece of the marquetry, inlay work or inlaid piece of coloured veneer.

When replacing an inlaid piece, proceed as per fitting a patch, except that here the piece has a shape determined by the pattern as well as a certain colour and quality

pyro–engraving tool (first try out the results on a piece of veneer you don't need).

11/ When replacing a patch of significant size set into an extensive surface, it is advisable to give it an irregular shape (straight edges are more difficult to blend in, the same with marrying up the grain).

On the whole, whenever the patch exceeds 2 or 3 cm on a side, it would be better to give the patch an irregular shape. The patch should be fitted following the same instructions as previously given.

12/ As it will normally be somewhat more difficult to make an irregular outline which exactly coincides with the area to be replaced, it is better to cut the veneer slightly oversize, lay it on the surface and, using a bradle, trace the outline of the piece so that it is marked out on the surface.

Then, remove the excess of the edges around the outline marked out and then fit the pre–glued replacement piece in, this will now fit perfectly.

Follow the normal procedure from here on in: leave to dry firmly clamped, etc.

perfectly.

This case in point is very often more likely to be found when the grain forms part of the circle obtained with four pieces cut one after the other from the same piece of wood.

To cover the cylindrical pieces of wood (pedestals of lamp stands, etc.), or other curved patterns for pieces of furniture, the traditional system consists of gluing the veneer strips in the cylindrical shape you need to cover.

To replace a damaged strip, it is probably easier to replace a complete one rather than just part.

Glue in place carefully and put a thin sheet of plastic over the veneer to protect it and to stop the glue oozing out sticking where it's not wanted.

Tie firmly in place without tightening too much (covering all the surface with previously moistened cord or string, depending on the

When the veneer which is to be replaced forms a pattern, (regularly fitting the feathers or circles which the wood's fibre has when the veneer has been cut on a knot or in the place where a branch has sprouted from the trunk), it may be necessary then to replace even the undamaged parts if no veneer can be found where the pattern matches up

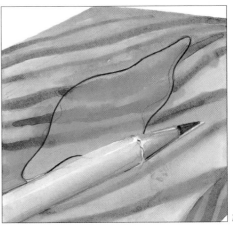

which contrast with its setting.

Ensure that the grain of the inlaid piece follows the same direction as corresponds (compare with the rest of the pattern).

Sometimes, each one of the pieces is edged by dark border (burnt or dyed), the simplest way of giving this finish to the new piece is to follow the edge with a felt tip pen of the same colour.

10/ In the event of wishing to lightly burn the edge, take great care to ensure that the sign doesn't intrude too far into the piece. Far better than a naked flame (from a candle, for instance), is to use the incandescent tip of a solder or

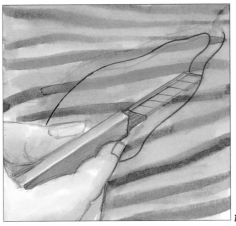

size of the column).

When the outer tying is dry, this will bring enormous pressure to bear (the cord used must be of natural fibre such as cotton, hemp, sisal, etc., never plastic).

Nowadays, using instant glue makes this procedure rather redundant except for certain cases.

REPLACING VENEERS. When dealing with large, very damaged surfaces, it is generally better to replace the entire veneer. If this is the option chosen, the first step is to remove all of the damaged surface veneer. It may also be advisable to veneer the top's underside to avoid curvature or warping of it by the different absorption of moisture on the two sides. On very extensive surfaces, it will be necessary to use more than one veneer and thus, we have detailed how to join the two sheets up.

When the surface area is curved, the procedure to follow will me the same for fitting a patch or covering a larger surface, but with the added difficulty of keeping the veneer and the base's surface well–joined with the help of clamps, shaped woods, etc.

1/ One system for removing veneer consists of dividing the surface up into areas by cutting the veneer with a scalpel or cutter. First, lightly press down with the blade and then apply more pressure gradually until the base wood is "felt" without actually harming it. To ensure that it comes off, it may be enough to simply rub carefully applying pressure all over the area using a steel ruler. Repeating this pressure makes the old glue come off and the piece comes away. Heat and humidity can also be used to help remove the veneer.

2/ Check that the veneer has been cut, then underneath the cut, gently insert a chisel or knife blade, carefully raising the veneer slowly.

Delicately tapping the chisel with a mallet will ensure that the veneer is raised enough to completely unstick it (pulling away with care) from the rest of the piece.

3/ When the entire veneer which has to be replaced has been pulled off, the old glue has to be cleaned off using hot water and a sponge or cotton cloth. Take care to ensure the water doesn't spread too far and gets underneath the veneer which doesn't need replacing (the undamaged edges).

The base surface must be left completely clean and smooth because any undulations will be passed on to the veneer and will be even more visible because of its shiny surface finish.

4/ Once the base is cleaned of all remains of old glue, the surface must be rubbed down using sandpaper to a perfect finish (the best way of applying even pressure which will leave a smooth, flat surface is to wrap the sandpaper around a wood block of suitable size to hold in your hand).

The rubbing down motion must be done in diagonal to the wood's fibre and when the cleaning process finishing, all traces of dust must be removed.

5/ There are currently two methods for artisanally fitting veneer: the traditional (using animal glue) or using the more modern synthetic adhesives (which are more often than not applied to the veneer and covered with a protective paper layer).

The latter system is cleaner and easier to glue: the veneer is cut to the right size, laid out on the surface (with the paper covered side up), and ironed over gently with a medium hot iron to first soften the glue.

6/ When the glue has cooled slightly, peel off the paper starting in one corner. Fit the veneer (with the glue bearing side toward the base surface). The paper removed is now used to cover the top of the veneer (to protect it), and the iron is once again employed on the veneer (medium hot), slowly advancing to ensure the glue melts and sticks gradually (without forming blisters). Do not overheat the glue and take care that the veneer doesn't slide owing to too much pressure being exerted.

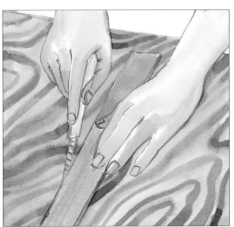

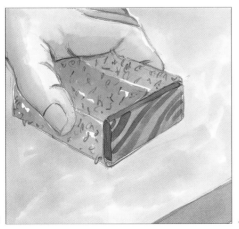

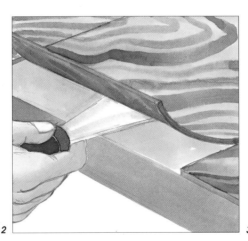

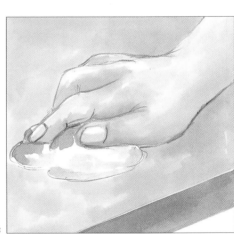

7/ Animal glue needs to be prepared prior to using it. Quarter fill the pot with glue flakes and then cover with hot water and leave to soften. Using a bain Marie, heat the pot to 49ºC (120ºF), until the mixture is of a soft, fluid consistency.

If treating a new surface, this must first have a water diluted mixture applied and then lightly rubbed down when dry. If a veneer has been removed, this preparatory step is not required.

8/ Apply an even thin coating of glue all over the base as well as on the reverse side of the veneer and leave aside until it is tacky to the touch.

Place the veneer in position and apply hand pressure to ensure that it is perfectly flat. Moisten the surface with a sponge (wetted with hot water and well squeezed first).

9/ Run a warm iron over all the moistened surface to help the glue to melt fully. Take particular care that the iron is not too hot as this will ruin the glue and the veneer will stick only partially.

10/ The end of the process consists of working with a veneer mallet in zigzag movements all along the fibre.

This will make excess glue or air pockets come out at the edges. If the glue crunches, it must be moistened and the veneer heated a little while working.

11/ When you need to join several sheets of veneer to cover the surface of a panel or tabletop, this must be done symmetrically, for instance, like the pages of an open book with the join in the middle of the surface. The two sheets are slightly overlapped (2.5

off the excess edging and rub down the edges so that they are rounded.

If the sheet is held up against a light bulb, there should be no light visible through the join. It can now be fitted as if it were one single sheet.

When it is dry, and if necessary, go over the edges with a blade or special saw for veneers to remove any projecting parts.

When a corner has to be repaired rounding off a top framed by a veneer strip, enough pieces of veneer must be cut (fan-shaped sections) so that when fitted one next to the other, they form a curve without changing the direction of the grain. Cut them a little oversize than needed so that they can then be adjusted outwards from one piece fitted in the centre of the curve. When they are stuck in place and dry, rectify

the excess part of the outer edge. On many pieces of furniture pieces, the veneer forms a rectangular frame with the corners mitred.

Cut the strip you wish to replace with the angle required so that it fits perfectly with the other one (check that the grain marries up properly), and glue having first used special adhesive tape for veneer or gummed paper to protect the edges (the adhesive on plastic tapes is too strong and may damage the veneer).

The paper strips are stuck on to stop air from getting in under the veneer and to keep the joins properly together (so that they don't separate when the glue dries).

The veneer mallet is very useful and is not used like a mallet, as its name first suggests, it is used to apply a firm, but light pressure on the surface of a recently glued on veneer, motion being applied in a zigzag from the centre outwards thereby ensuring that the excess glue comes out and stops bubbles forming.

7

8

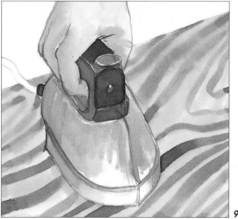

9

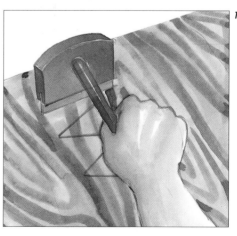

10

cm). Place a ruler in the centre of the overlapping part and cut through the two layers of veneer at the same time using a very sharp blade, if possible in one go and, if the join is very long, using short, firm cuts.

Remove the strip cut off from the overlapping sheet as well as the other one, always taking care that the sheets do not move.

Moisten and iron the join so that it joins (fit the two properly straight edges together), smooth down using the veneer mallet or roller and fix the join with insulating tape or gummed paper so that the edges are kept fully in contact while drying.

12/ When the join is dry, turn the veneer over (good side down) on a flat true surface, cut

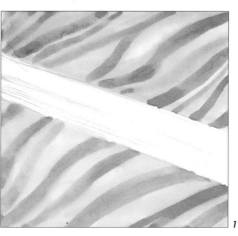

11

12

REPLACING BROKEN PARTS. Seriously damaged or broken mouldings and edgings only have one solution: replace the damaged parts with patches.

If the section is rather large, it may be better to replace the entire moulding *(buying the amount required with an equal or very similar pattern)*. Nevertheless, if the piece of furniture is valuable, this must be conserved as close to original as possible, thus one or several patches –the smaller, the better– should provide the best solution.

1/ Start by cutting off the damaged section, making the cut in dovetail so that later on, the new piece will be firmly glued in place. The new piece should be cut from wood matching the original as closely as possible insofar as grain and fibre alike. It is not necessary to give the piece shape yet, merely that it fits well on the edges. Glue and leave to dry.

2/ If the mould's shape allows it and it has flat sides, the fitted piece can be roughed down using a plane. If the piece has curved surfaces or a more complex profile, shape must be given by carving it using chisels of the right size.

3/ When giving a curved shape, the chisel must be used with great care so as not to take off too much wood.

The final finish will always be done by rubbing down.

4/ To copy complex mouldings, the best solution is to make an exact copy of the profile by hollowing out a block of wood. This hollow block will then be covered with fine grade sandpaper and be passed repeatedly over the length of the moulding until it has been brought down to match the rest. To make the end result indistinguishable,

the wood must be coloured and given the appropriate finish. One trick for getting a well–defined pattern consists of rubbing the moulding with a piece of hard wood which will define and harden the edges, giving a better appearance to the repair.

5/ Faults or breakages in the wood of flat surfaces may also appear.

A straight-sided patch could well be the solution for a hole or deep burn. The patch is cut and prepared from a wood closely

Sometimes, it is useful to try a corner of the wood, giving it the finish which it will later be given (or a fine coat of lacquer) to see and compare the wood's final appearance (the refractive index, tonality, etc.), prior to deciding to cut the patch.

When it isn't possible to match up the grain, that part of the grain with swirls formed by a knot in the wood can be chosen, but this option, obviously, can only be taken if there are others similar elsewhere on the piece of furniture and it doesn't degrade the beauty of the board.

6/ With the chisel well–sharpened, make the hole as deep as is required and level off the bottom so that the patch fits perfectly.

The patch will always be a little thicker than the depth of the hole (it's easier to rub down the insert than having it sunken in the hole), and this will be given the same shape as the hole –either rhomboid or oval, like the deck of a ship– we have already stated that these shapes are the easiest ones to match up with the grain and cloak the joins.

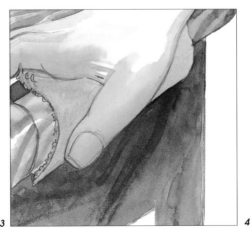

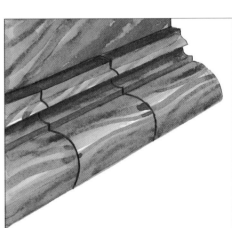

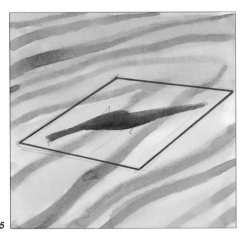

matching the original surface as possible. Pay attention to the flow and quantity of the grain's lines and try to ensure they match up as best possible.

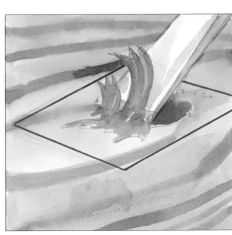

7/ If, in addition, the surface is veneered, the patch must be double: the first will be inserted into the base wood (with the grain in the same direction because it will then work and move the same as the base, ensuring that it won't come unstuck or jut out making it visible), followed by the veneer.

For the surface veneer, prepare a rhomboid (in this case) the same as that of the base wood, but slightly larger than the base when this has fully dried and has been levelled off flush with the surface. Now fit the veneer patch (as per instructions on page 50 and following).

The patch must always be cut and bevelled a little on the edges to ensure that it enters under pressure and thus stays more firmly in place.

almost infinite and the technique to use will also vary as well as the kind of patch to use,

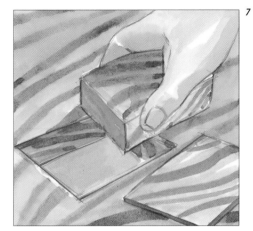

Whenever possible, the piece of wood used should be given the appropriate form so that the glue is enough in itself to keep it in place. If the part to which the patch has been fitted has been left weakened by the repair, it is advisable to fit some kind of bracing underneath (not visible) which will be fitted with nails: holes are made in the wood and base, the nails are glued and inserted into the suitably cleaned, lightly glued holes, then driven home gently until fully home and then left to dry.

Lastly, the part jutting out of each nail is cut off and the brace is applied, the same finish as the base is put on so that it blends in as much as possible.

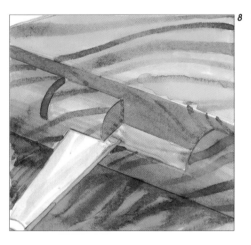

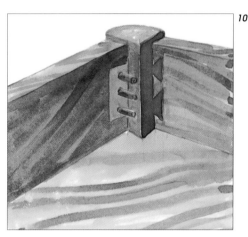

8/ Very often, only the upper part of the rounded edge of a surface is damaged and it's a pity to replace all of the moulding's thickness.

We have already recommended looking for the right kind of repair which ensures that the minimum of the original piece of furniture is removed. It is enough, therefore, to repair the top of the moulding in this case.

The method to use here consists of making some cuts every few centimetres (using a small fretsaw) down to the depth you wish to replace.

Then, with the help of a chisel, remove the bits of wood marked out, leaving a smooth surface behind at the same level all over where the patch is to be fitted.

9/ Select the strips of wood, if possible of the same type or of a similar hardness at least (similar fibre, grain and colour, etc.), and cut the appropriate piece to glue in place over the prepared moulding section. Fit firmly in place using clamps until the adhesive is dry and then shape accordingly.

There are small-sized planes which have the right blades to give the shape corresponding to the most widely used mouldings.

These make it much easier to blend the patch in with the rest of the moulding. Nevertheless, with a bit of patience and care, a chisel can also give good results.

10/ Those cases which may arise when patches are fitted to repair breakages in several parts of a piece of furniture, are

etc. Generally speaking, all repairs which are visible and use nails or metal pieces which were not used in the piece of furniture's construction, are considered to be "cowboy" and are better off being replaced by another, more proper one.

REMOVAL OF OPAQUE PAINTS. There will always be pieces of furniture which need a total renovation of the finish, particularly the paintwork. It just isn't feasible to go on applying coat after coat on the piece: there comes a time when it's simply impossible to open or close the doors or drawers, the surfaces are also left uneven to the touch owing to the differing thicknesses of the successive coats. Nothing is worse than chipped paint revealing the colour of the finish underneath.

However, it is always advisable to first give the top coat a good clean prior to stripping of the old paint. If the dirt layer is not too heavy, use a three parts water one part vinegar solution. If, however, the dirt is significant, use 50 g of detergent in a litre of hot water. Use a sponge (well–squeezed) on the surfaces, leave the solution to work in for around ten minutes and repeat if necessary. Do not allow the surface layer to become overly wet as water could get through cracks or splits in the paint and damage the wood. When dealing with complex mouldings or carvings, use an old toothbrush or shaving brush. The process should always be finished off by removing the solution and grime and then drying the surface with cloths *(cotton preferably)*. There are a series of safety rules which must be taken into consideration prior to starting to strip off old paint *(and other finishes too)*. Use a well–ventilated room *(you will be using inflammable products and if doing the work outdoors, these could possibly be exposed to sunlight)*. The floor should be anti–slip to avoid accidents while working with toxic products which could cause serious burns. It is better that the piece of furniture being worked on is kept close to the floor, this is because the toxic fumes tend to gravitate downwards and keeping the piece of furniture close to the floor will allow the restorer to breathe cleaner air, better yet if the restorer uses a mask covering nose and mouth. If there is no mains water tap close by, prepare a container holding enough water to quickly rinse off any splashes.

The restorer should wear protective eyewear *(even fumes can cause harm to the eyes)*. Strong, thick rubber gloves *(better if the arms are also covered)*. A working apron or similar *(it is advisable to wear old clothes underneath which cover and protect well and it will not matter if they become stained)*. Smoking is strictly prohibited while stripping the paint off the piece of furniture. It is also advisable to keep all persons not involved in the job away from the workplace, children, animals, pregnant women and the elderly in particular *(or anyone who tends to suffer from breathing difficulties)*.

If you are going to spend a long time or several days even –breaks included– exposed to the toxic fumes of solvents, it is essential to use a breathing mask or, better still, a good respirator with filter. Applying the solvent using a spray gun is not recommended, this includes commercially available solvents in aerosols, as they are quite difficult to control.

The risk of fire is very real so avoid working close to light sources, etc.

It is advisable to have a fire extinguisher to hand when undertaking paint stripping work.

Buying the right amount of product you are going to use is the best bet, storing unused inflammable products for any length of time greatly enhances the fire risk *(temperature changes, etc., may cause their spontaneous combustion)*. A good way of getting rid of any possible solvent remains, as well as the treated paint stripped off the piece of furniture, is to leave it to evaporate or dry outdoors inside old containers until what is left solidifies *(in safe places out of the reach of children and animals and away from fire)*, then, take said containers to a suitable disposal site. When using prepared solvents, rigorously follow the instructions given by the maker.

If these don't specify anything to the contrary, this means that they can be used for all wood types and for stripping the majority of paints or finishes.

*1/ **If the piece of furniture is covered with thick** coats of paint, remove doors and drawers which will be dealt with separately. Gradually strip off the old paint, moving the piece of furniture so that the surface being dealt with is always horizontal.*
Pour out the stripper into a small plastic pot which has a lid.
Apply using a very broad brush (when the paint is very thick, it may be necessary to wrap the piece of furniture in sheets of plastic or moistened sacks so that the stripper does not dry out and continues acting longer. This system is even more essential when dealing with complex mouldings and carvings).
***2/ When the solvent product has done its work (**a process needing a set time and cannot be hurried), remove the sheets covering the piece of furniture and rinse down with a copious water jet. Use a spatula to remove the paint from the flat surfaces of the piece of furniture. Continue cleaning off the remains of paint left behind using medium–thick wire wool. There are always*

nooks and crannies where the solvent has not been able to properly soften the paint and which will have to be cleaned with care using a blade.
3/ Another system for stripping opaque paint *off is the one using caustic soda. This is a spectacularly efficient method for large pieces, but one which does carry certain problems with it.*

It must be used outdoors and always with hosepipe close to hand (any splashes can be rinsed off using copious amounts of water).
As is the case with working with other chemical solvents, protective clothing, eyewear and plastic (not rubber) gloves should be worn and, despite taking all of these precautions, the risk of being burned is still very high, in particular to someone not used to working continually with this method.
There are other products besides caustic soda which are effective: potash, the powders used to unblock drains, etc.
A handful in a litre of water will give you a ready–made preparation for stripping paint.
A paste can also be made by adding flour and stirring until it thickens.
Apply using a scouring pad or sponge.
The foam it produces means that the chemical product is taking effect. If nothing happens, add more water and wait.

4

5

while cherry changes to reddish).
It may also be necessary to rub the piece of furniture down prior to applying a new finish.
To sum up: a highly effective procedure, but not very advisable for delicate or valuable pieces of furniture.

7/ A final piece of advice for the amateur
restorer: it may be best to use a commercial paint stripper (though it be slower and mean more work), closely following the maker's instructions.
To summarise the whole process, the following illustration is given: application of product, elimination of softened paint, eliminate paint remains using steel wool, cleaning down and rinsing off of the product remains and, lastly, rubbing the wood down.

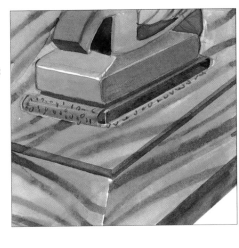

7

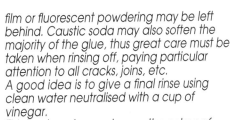

6

film or fluorescent powdering may be left behind. Caustic soda may also soften the majority of the glue, thus great care must be taken when rinsing off, paying particular attention to all cracks, joins, etc.
A good idea is to give a final rinse using clean water neutralised with a cup of vinegar.
This treatment may change the colour of some woods (oak and chestnut darken

4/ To accelerate the process, scrub with a brush. Do not allow the treated surface to dry out (a watering can or spray can be used to wet).
When dealing with curved surfaces, it is better to help the process along using a hard brush or blunt blade (taking care to not leave any marks on the wood).
Finally, rinse off using copious amounts of water and continue repeating the process on those areas which have not been treated in the first application.
5/ Another variation on the same technique consists of a uniform sprinkling of the caustic soda crystals directly onto the surface to be stripped.
Pour very hot water directly over the surface (using a watering can with fine holes).
This will cause instantaneous effervescence (take great care with the fumes given off, these are usually very toxic). If necessary, repeat the treatment.
6/ After these treatments using caustic soda or suchlike, the piece of furniture must be thoroughly washed down.
If the rinsing off is not done properly, a thin

In some cases, the paint may be in such a bad state (full of chips and peeling off), that it may be best to simply try removing it with a scraper (do not confuse this with a pasting trowel). Nevertheless, it is still necessary to take great care not to scratch or damage the wood as later on this incur more work in trying to hide the marks with fillers prior to applying the new finish. (These repairs are detailed on page 35).
In nooks and crannies difficult to reach using the scraper, a knife blade or cutter can be used. Mechanical sanders are, in theory, ideal for paint stripping work but, in reality, remove the old paint in a haphazard fashion and can quite easily score or mark the wood. Another alternative procedure is to scrape off using heat. This is very fast but highly dangerous for the piece of furniture.
The restorer applies heat using the blow torch in one hand and scrapes the heated area with a scraper in the other.
Any distraction, however, means that the wood will be burnt or that hot paint shavings could burn the restorer. This system is only really of use for flat surfaces as it will always burn the outermost part of anything in relief when trying to soften up paint in the nooks and crannies.
Aqueous–based solvents are not so toxic, nor as quick –taking several hours or overnight even to soften the paint. This lengthy period of time with moisture present may raise the woodgrain (swelling) thereby occasioning a more intense rubbing down afterwards.
A paste solvent could well work better given that it stays put without dripping or running, even when applied on vertical surfaces.
If the piece of furniture has a surface not requiring stripping, cover this totally with insulating tape.

REMOVAL OF TRANSPARENT FINISHES. Comment has already been made that removing the original finish on antique furniture is a great shame indeed, particularly if this is a bodied–up rubber lacquer. This kind of finish is quite unusual to find today and, for this reason alone, would be a crying shame to do away with it. The "crime" would be of further compounded if, in addition, the idea is to replace it with a common–or–garden synthetic varnish. Sometimes, however, the state of the varnish is so deplorable that there is no other remedy but to repair it, removing it being a necessity to then go on to reapply a new coat of it, or a similar type of finish. It may be interesting to first know how to identify the kind of finish which has to be removed from a piece of furniture, given that the product to be used to do so will have to be different. It will also be necessary to know whether the new finish to be applied once the stripping and preparation work has been done, is going to be the same or different.

LACQUER *(or French polishing, etc.)*, gives a thin, translucid gloss finish. It looks like glass and no marks from rubbing down or the brush, etc., appear on it. The problem with this kind of finish is that it is vulnerable and doesn't stay in good shape for very long: it breaks down with heat to form whitish opaque stains. If water has been spilt on it without being mopped up and dried immediately, the area affected is ruined *(by a white, semi–transparent gloss)*.

Scratches and scoring scale off at the edges and take on a whitish–yellow colouring. The majority of antique furniture were given this finish. To find out if this is so, apply a drop of methyl–alcohol on a non–visible part of the pieces and see if the varnish loses its shine.

1/ To remove lacquer French polishing, proceed gradually, treating a small area and, once clean, go on to the next one. When carrying out this job, take the usual precautions when working with toxic, highly inflammable products (page 56). At the very least, choose a well–ventilated place (windows fully open), put paper down on the floor, put rubber gloves and protective eyewear on to prevent eye irritation. Denaturalised alcohol, strong ammonia liquid or a suitable paint solvent can be used. Given that all of these products give off unpleasant fumes (the lesser evil being possibly alcohol here), apply only a drop at a time on the area being worked on.

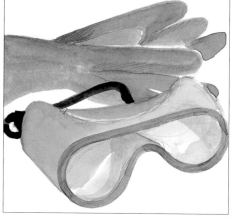

2/ Rub the finish using a piece of fine steel wool (it is better that the area be small, around finger size) until a light "sauce" appears.

The ball of steel wool must always be moved along the grain, never across it or in circles. The "sauce" means that the finish is dissolving (breaking down). Take advantage of this moment to quickly remove it using absorbent cloths, cotton wool or paper (whatever you use, it's better if it's white and clean).

A practical idea would be to use toilet paper because it can be picked up easily even with rubber gloves on. Continue removing the dissolved lacquer until the paper or cloth is still clean after rubbing on the area.

Leave to dry and continue as before.

If wishing to give this writing desk, made and enhanced by Ateliers Gelea, a new appearance, it would first be a good idea to remove the varnished finish, leaving visible the wood's natural grain under the soft sheen of the varnish and give it a new finish, which will highlight its stylish Empire lines, with a beautiful ebony imitation patina.

VARNISH is a longer lasting, hardwearing finish than lacquer.

If the piece of furniture is examined carefully, it may be the case that the brush has not touched all the nooks and crannies equally, forming varnish runs or drips. Another detail to look for is to closely examine any scratches or marks (the edges will not be like those found on lacquer) and, in general, if the finish is in relatively good condition despite intense use, if this is so then the finish is in all probability varnished.

If a small amount of methyl alcohol is applied on to the finish and this doesn't change, then it is varnish.

Mineral oil or turpentine, on the other hand, will tend to soften it.

4/ Varnish stripping work is a great deal simpler on the flat surfaces of modern pieces of furniture.

When the restorer has to work with mouldings, carvings or turnings, the process becomes somewhat more complex, and inventiveness and imagination have to be brought to bear to reach into the remotest nook or cranny.
A toothbrush can give a soft scrubbing action on the sunken parts of mouldings where it would be awkward to reach with a larger brush or wire wool.

5/ If stripping off the grooves of a turned leg with a pointed instrument (needle or suchlike), it is more than likely that the only result will be badly scratched wood which is not even clean. If you wrap a piece of string with a bit of fine steel wool, this will enable you to reach even the most hidden parts of the turning.

Hold one end of the string in each hand and move in a shoe buffing motion.

Cotton cords and toothpicks can also become useful tools for reaching right into the tiniest nooks and crannies and slots difficult to reach otherwise.

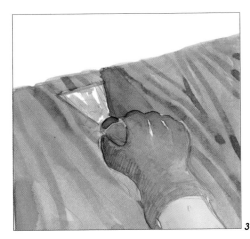

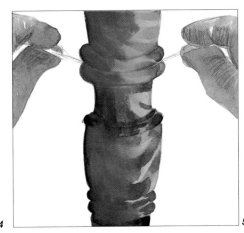

3/ When you don't know what kind of varnish has been used for the finish you want to remove (particularly if the piece of furniture isn't very old), you'll have to try different products until finding the right one.

It is important to follow the order given here: turpentine, denaturalised alcohol, commercial paint solvents, acetone, ammonia, caustic soda and a strong borax solution. These are applied with an old brush onto a non-visible part of the finish which is then rubbed or scraped with wire wool or a scraper.

Always remember that all rubbing must follow the line of the grain.

Having decided upon the product which works the best, it is better to use it gradually in stages on the piece of furniture.

Remember that all products, liquid or not, spread better and work best on horizontal surfaces, thus, whenever possible, turn the piece to enable this.

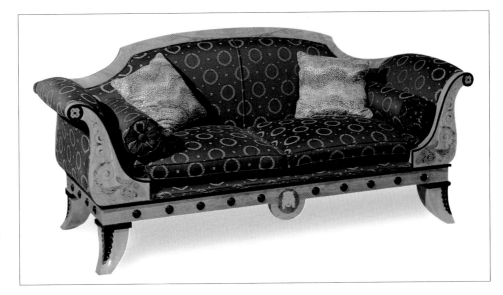

If you decide to renovate the upholstery of the settee (Made by Época), this light-coloured finish with bare wood is probably not the most appropriate one, better to remove it prior to giving it a different one.

If you aren't sure of the kind of finish you're going to remove, it must be stressed that, as is the case for paint stripping, it is better to try out different kinds of solvents *(in a non-visible place on the piece of furniture, just in case the wood or its natural colouring is damaged)*, and choose the one which works best with the minimum possible stress to the piece of furniture's wood. Simplifying the procedure and the amount of tools needed as much as possible, the process can be summarised in a few steps.

It will always be better to try to do the job in the simplest way which is least destructive to the piece of furniture. When the result obtained is not good enough or the surfaces to treat are too large, that is the time to resort to more demanding remedies.

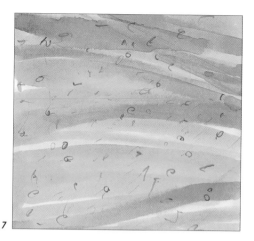

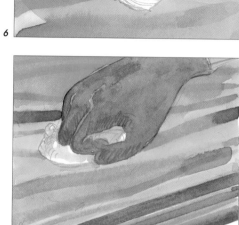

6/ Spread a generous coat of the chosen stripper and wait a moment. Almost immediately, bubbles of some sort will begin to appear showing the effectiveness of the product.

7/ When the stripper has stopped bubbling, but the surface still appears wet, vigorously rub using coarse steel wool in all directions. This step removes the greater part of the varnish.

8/ Clean the surface off with a little water

(unless the maker's instructions state otherwise), and if necessary, rub again with clean steel wool (finer than the previous). Next, rub over with a cotton cloth.

9/ To remove the last vestiges of varnish, rub over with sandpaper until the surface on which the treatment for the new finish is to be applied to, is left smooth.

This magnificent Época make drum bureau was hidden under several coats of paint. After being fully stripped down and a new finish applied, it has been completely restored to its former splendour.

To recognise a _WAXED_ finish, bear in mind that it can be scratched and marked with a finger nail.
If subjected to heat, it will break down and take on a whitish, chipped and opaque appearance.
A waxed finish is one of the most attractive and pleasing around.
Although it is delicate, it can always be repaired by using a little wax and rubbing...(_a waxed finish whose sheen has dimmed can be reanimated immediately by rubbing it over with a slow drying wax or a cloth moistened with a few drops of turpentine_).
Sometimes, the wax can build up into a thick layer and accumulate so much dirt that it is necessary to remove it and reapply wax or apply a different finish.
The best system to use is a special commercial cleaner for wax finishes. Denaturalised alcohol, methyl alcohol or white spirit must never be used, as these products could alter the finish of the paint or varnish which is to be subsequently applied.
This precaution is even more necessary if a water–based paint finish is going to be applied.
CELLULOSE–based varnishes are hard and difficult to mark.
They are usually found on modern day furniture forming a fragile, glasslike film.
This finish doesn't dissolve with either turpentine or any alcohol.
To soften it, resort must be made to commercial solvents for cellulose paints.
Another finish which gives a beautiful, but short lasting, shine is that given by VARNISH and LINSEED oil.
When this finish is dirty and dull, it can be easily restored by rubbing with turpentine and linseed oil.
The greater part of the polish is found below the wood's surface (_it penetrates deeply into the wood's fibres_).
To restore it, rub it at any angle or in circles with a moistened pad and then clean the area with boiled linseed oil.
This will restore the finish and remove the marks, but not for any great length of time as the result is not long lasting.

10

11

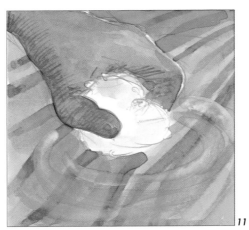

12

10/ Immerse a fine scouring pad in the wax stripper and rub the surface using circular movements. Work gradually ensuring that all layers of the wax, right down to the deepest one, are removed.
11/ Remains of old wax can be removed with a cloth and, if necessary, apply more stripper and continue rubbing. The surface must be left completely free of any vestiges of wax. Obviously, this process is more arduous in corners, carvings and mouldings. The same or similar tricks as those suggested for the removal of other finishes can likewise be used here.
12/ Rub the entire surface with fine sandpaper. The surface must be left with a softness which allows a good result to be obtained when applying the preliminary treatment for the new finish.

There are finishes which have a painted base and are then decorated with stencilling, "découpage," patterning or enriched with hand painted flowers, grecques or figures which are protected with a transparent finish that may be in bad condition.
If wishing to remove the finish to renovate it but without losing the decorative element, the job then assumes a delicate nature.
In such cases, removal of the damaged finish has to be superficial only, at least in the decorated parts with the immediate application of a transparent finish.
When the damaged parts also affect the paintwork, you must be prepared to faithfully reproduce any detail erased or damaged.

A wax finish, with its soft deep sheen, highlights the quality of the bronze appliques of this chest of drawers made by Geka.

BLEACHING AND RUBBING DOWN. After stripping, of both paint and transparent finishes and prior to beginning the actual preparation for the new finish, it may be necessary to carry out a bleaching process. In some cases, owing to the original colouring or the ravages of time on some kinds of wood (*oak, walnut, etc.*), this may have acquired too dark a colour for the new finish. It may also be the case that, on removing the finish, old dye stains, glass circles and other faults come to light. These can be treated individually as stains (*with a little bleach, etc., see page 38*), or carry out a general bleaching.

The easiest route is to use commercial wood bleaches, sodium hypochlorite or crystallised oxalic acid. Just as using bleaches for clothes, cleaning, etc. in the home carries a certain risk with it by improper usage, so it is with wood bleaches too. These are very strong indeed and have to be stored out of the reach of children. When using these preparations wear protective eyewear and gloves, cover yourself with suitable clothing and work in a well–ventilated place, better yet, out of doors. It is advisable to work close to a water tap or have a container of water to hand to immediately rinse any splashes off.

*1/ **Add the crystals to water in the ratio of 30 g** per 0.3 litres. Apply using an old brush or sponge, taking care that the product acts uniformly.*

Afterwards, wash with a solution of 30 g of borax to half a litre of water and wipe well. Leave to dry for 24 hours.

Another bleaching process is to use a one part ammonia (of 0.88) to five parts water. This should also be applied with an old brush and washed off with water and hydrogen peroxide. One part hydrogen peroxide (of 100 volumes) to two parts water.

This process could remove the reddish hue of mahogany.

On the whole, proceed with great caution

and if possible, gradually. All bleaching agents are strong chemically and some very toxic indeed.

Prior to starting the general bleaching process *of a piece of furniture, you must first consider not only if it is advisable, but also whether it is absolutely necessary.*

This is a process which is easy to apply on large surfaces but becomes somewhat finicky when applying to mouldings, carvings, etc., and which may completely remove the wood's patina.

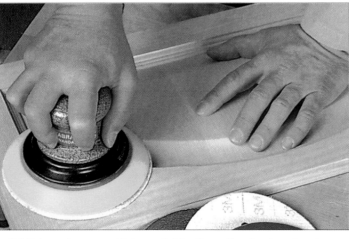

Orbital sanders are widely available. The self-adhesive abrasive and sail type strips are designed to be positioned quickly and firmly on the flat base. When hand sanding with paper-based abrasives, products with aluminium mineral oxide work well on all kinds of wood and suchlike surfaces. Eccentric sanding machines (roto-orbital), are becoming ever-increasingly popular. This tool is suitable for intermediate and finishing sanding on both wood and lacquers alike.

2/ Commercial wood bleaches are usually comprised of two products which are applied separately.

The first one is applied with a brush onto the surface being bleached.

Care must be taken to spread it evenly over the surface, without splashing adjacent areas or allowing the product to run.

After roughly 20 minutes (the wood will have gradually darkened during this time), the second product is applied (another brush must be used here).

3/ Always follow the maker's instructions, but

5/ If you only want to bleach a part of the piece of furniture, the wood adjacent to this area must first be protected with insulating tape, then proceed as previously explained but taking greater care not to splash those parts you want to keep as they are.

6/ Whichever bleaching process you have used, all of them involve the wetting of the wood with the ensuing swelling of its fibres. Once fully dried out, the surface must be rubbed down (with greater or lesser intensity depending on the finish process chosen).

To manually rub a surface down, we have

7/ The initial passes must applied at an angle to the grain, never along it or across it.

The motion used must be applied gently and uniformly.

Always end using a finer grade paper, with the rubbing motion gradually coming into line with the fibre, ending up by being in parallel with the grain.

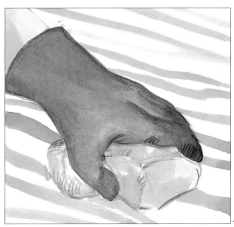

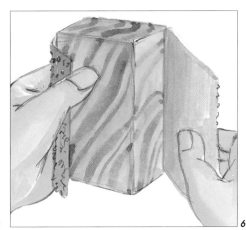

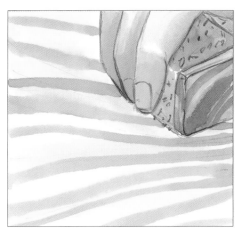

as a rule, four hours after applying the second product, the desired colour should now have been obtained.

Wash the wood with a weak solution of acetic acid (a teaspoonful of vinegar in a good-sized glass of water).

4/ The natural colour of woods changes radically with bleaching.

As examples of those woods which can take on an attractive colouring using this process, the cases of American Oak, Cherry and Mahogany are noteworthy of mention.

The process must always be interrupted when the colour is slightly darker than that desired finally (the wood will take on a lighter hue on drying). If, after finishing the operation, the colour is still too dark, the process can be repeated without any problems.

already recommended the usage of a block of wood (or cork) which fits comfortably in your hand, and which is covered with the abrasive paper.

Electric sanders (using sandpaper) are suitable for large surfaces and fast sanding down, or when dealing with removing material in even amounts.

However, for small or intricate jobs or for surfaces with a lot of shapes, hand sanding is the best method to use, use a block of wood covered with sandpaper which is suited to the surface being sanded.

For other kinds of surfaces such as mouldings or the sunken parts of turnings, the best bet is to use the sandpaper folded.

When working in tight corners or on minute details, cover the tip of a wooden rod with a strip of sandpaper.

Normal practice is to first use a coarse grade sandpaper finishing off with a fine grade.

TREATMENTS. Once the finish has been finally removed and any vestiges of the products used have been neutralised, the piece of furniture will, in all probability, have a dull tarnished appearance. A faint mottling of the surface caused by the slight accumulation of dirt is actually allowable, if you think that it will give a certain patina to the finish which is to be subsequently applied.

1/ However, if you prefer to start out working with a clean piece of furniture, wash it down with a solution of oxalic acid.
(As is normal when handling a dangerous product, the wearing of appropriate gloves, apron and respiratory mask and protective eyewear is a necessity).
Half fill a glass container with hot water and gradually add the oxalic acid crystals taking care while doing so –never pour the hot water over the crystals, always the other way round– Add the crystals using dry spatula until no further crystals are dissolved, the solution is now saturated. Leave to stand for ten minutes prior to using it.

2/ There are surfaces with no finish or some which even after stripping have an oily greasy surface (an old kitchen table, for instance).
Stripping will temporarily solve the problem by eliminating the dark impregnation existing underneath, but the stain will reappear within a few days and will exude oil or grease.
Should eliminating the impregnated oil prove impossible, this will have to be stabilised to stop it coming through the new finish. Take the piece of furniture outdoors and wash down thoroughly with petrol applied using steel wool to remove the oil or grease insofar as is possible (taking all the usual safety precautions: appropriate gloves, apron, do not inhale fumes, do not smoke).
To stabilise the oil, a small quantity of high

1

2

quality varnish (not polyurethane based), mineral turpentine and some paint drying agents are needed.
Dissolve a tablespoonful of varnish in a container of distilled mineral turpentine, then add a teaspoonful of drying agent.
Wash the surface with this mixture and wipe off shortly afterwards.
Leave to dry and repeat the operation on several successive days. The piece of furniture must be rubbed down lightly between coats.
Gradually add more varnish each time while reducing the amounts of mineral turpentine and drying agent. When the amounts of turpentine and drying agent are minimal, application of the definitive finish can now be commenced, if this process is not followed, the final finish will not harden properly. If it is, the final varnishing will be smooth and shiny. Waxing and rubbing will give an intense shine.

After stripping down and leaving the piece of furniture's wood bare, now is the time to repair any other problems such as gluing (which may have been weakened by the products used in this process), breakages of the wood, add new parts, etc., which will now be easier to match up when applying a new finish.

The intact appearance of this bureau's finish did not impede having had to treat the wood in order for the final result to be perfect prior to its application. Made by Época.

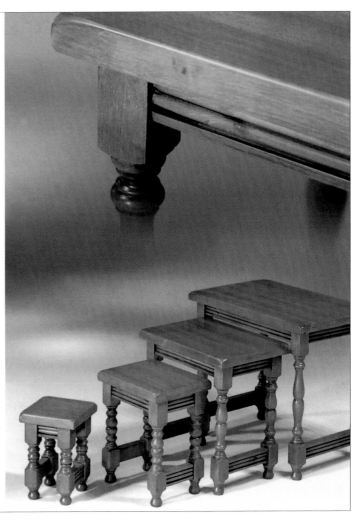

Knots very often appear in solid wood which spoil the finish.
With the right treatment, this problem can be avoided (Toledart).

3/ If you have to apply a finish (varnish or
paint) to a piece of furniture which has had
surfaces covered with linoleum, oilcloth or
other impermeable materials, the problems
arising when having to remove them can be
rather testing for the restorer's skills and
patience.
The first step consists of unsticking the material
from its backing surface using manual means
(scraping, pulling off, levering off or cutting
with the aid of a chisel).
Scraping the surface to remove all of the
adhesive, leaving it clean except for some
vestiges of old glue. To remove them, use a
stripper or resort, if need be, to using petrol
or other more toxic solvents (always
taking all necessary precautions and carrying
out the operation out of doors to minimise
fumes).
When the piece of furniture is clean and
ready, now is the time to apply any treatment
its wood may require: anti-woodworm,
anti-rot (dry or wet), as well as examining in
detail all surfaces to be given a finish.
You'll have to remove any marks or stains
which may have been made when removing
the finish or which we already there on the
piece of furniture, match up the grain, etc.
4/ It may be necessary to treat resinous knots
(these may subsequently appear as defects
in whatever finish is applied), particularly

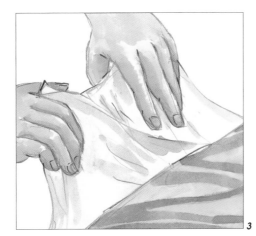
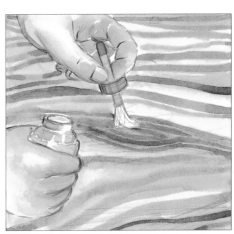

natural knots which appear in the new parts
of repaired pieces of furniture.
Pine and other softwoods may exude resin
even to the point of staining and coming
through varnished or painted finish.
A lacquer-based sealant is the solution to this
problem.
Apply two coats of the product which can be
bought already prepared in hardware shops
(leaving enough drying time between coats).
The container will generally have a brush for
applying the product attached inside the
top.

Woods which in their time were considered too
simple to wear a transparent finish and which
were painted, are usually stripped back to
their base and given a transparent finish.
It is worthwhile, therefore, to get a quality
base treatment appropriate for the new finish
chosen.

FILLING PORES. After stripping paint off or bleaching the wood, it will be necessary to fill in the wood's pores to give it a perfect surface prior to the application of rubber lacquer or varnishing it. Dying can be done either before or after filling the pores, all depending on the case in question.

Some finishes: ageing, dying or surface dressing *(with linseed oil, teak oil, wax or petroleum jelly)*, base their effect on the grain being visible, thus primers or base coats must never be used.

1/ There are ready made pore filling products available, however, should you wish to use to determined colour it will probably be better to make one yourself.

Add the powder pigmented to the colour you want to plaster of Paris (normally brown Van Dick powder for dark oak and red ochre for mahogany). When you want the grain to stand out in white through the varnish, do not use pigments.

2/ Spread pigmented (or not) plaster onto a damp cloth, apply onto the wood using a circular motion which fills the grain and end up rubbing along the grain.

Leave to dry. Check to see that the pores have been filled by passing your hand over the surface which should feel really smooth. If this is not the case, repeat the filling process. When completely dry, smooth down using a very fine grade abrasive paper, rubbing along the grain.

3/ One method ideally suited for French polished lacquer finishes, is to use pumice stone powder. The powder is sieved and a clean pad of white cotton cloth is wetted with denaturalised alcohol.

Dip this pad into the sieved pumice stone powder and cover the entire surface by

first, and then along the grain), the surface must be treated in sections given that when dry, it is difficult to remove any excess.

5/ Wait approximately 15 minutes and remove any excess filler.

When the surface is flat, use a scraper, if it is smaller or has mouldings, a strip of hessian or sackcloth.

6/ On corners and slots, it is better to use a pointed peg wrapped in a bit of cloth (if a

metal instrument is used, the wood runs the risk of being scored).

The cloth has to be changed whenever it becomes saturated with filler.

Another preparation which used to be applied to Italian furniture in the 18th century to hide the wood's roughness or bad quality, was Italian lacquer. The basis of this procedure consists in dissolving several leaves of rabbit-foot in a bain Marie and apply this lacquer using a hard brush. It is then left to dry overnight.

The mixture is prepared of 170 g of powdered kaolin in one litre of white casein, to which is added 70 g of casein emulsion, three drops of pine oil, 1.25 cc of ox bile, 1.25 cc of fungicide crushed in 2.5 cc of water and 360 cc of water.

This is then filtered (using a fine mesh and helped through with a hard brush).

The resulting thick cream is applied in a minimum of eight coats, leaving enough drying time between them as well as rubbing down before applying the next one.

The end finish is comprised of several coats of lacquer, etc.

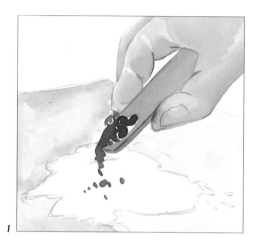

gently rubbing evenly in small circles. The grain is thus entirely covered in all directions. If the area to treat is large, shake the pad out and refold it to give a fresh clean face to continue rubbing.

4/ To get a very fine surface finish on open-pore woods (like oak, mahogany, ash or walnut), the filler can also be applied using a brush. In tight-grained woods (pine, birch, maple, cherry, etc.), as well as when wishing to achieve a rustic or rural appearance,

it isn't necessary to apply fillers onto the wood itself, but you will have to apply it on joins or where there are imperfections. It has a thick creamy consistence and is applied using a hard brush (in diagonal cross strokes

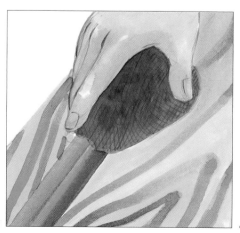

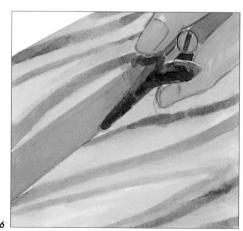

DYING. Dying wood can be done for two different reasons: to match the new parts to the original piece of furniture, or to give it a new appearance. Woods which are more than fifty or sixty years old have a much richer colour than recently sawn ones. This darkening effect is not just superficial and gives qualities of lustre and shine that cannot be imitated by dying, except in very small areas. If abundant dye is applied, the wood will darken unevenly and the dye will tend to create a barrier of pigments which tarnish and destroy its reflective qualities.

1/ When simply wishing to darken the too–new wood of a piece of furniture, the best method is to fade using ammonia gas. This is an extremely toxic product, the inhalation of which may cause temporary blindness and respiratory problems. Handling this product requires taking a great many precautions and is best done out of doors. Oak and chestnut are woods rich in tannins and can be treated directly, other

–taking great care– in the bag which must then be immediately sealed using adhesive tape.

3/ Fading is also used to colour wood newly joined to old. For instance, if the original oak wood of a leg is already very dark, it will not be affected by exposure to fumes as the new part will be.
When dealing with other woods needing to be impregnated with tannic or pyrogallic acid, only the treated parts will be directly affected by the ammonia fumes.

4/ Dying is a simple way of transforming and protecting the wood. There are several techniques according to the dilutant used: water, oil, alcohol, etc.
To dye water, dissolve the powdered colours in it (fabric dyes, alcohol dyes or powder pigments can be used, all are effective and allow a wide range of colours to be obtained).
Always try out the dye on a piece of wood prior to deciding the definitive mix.
To begin: mix a spoonful of liquid dye in half a litre of water. Next, add more water or dye until the desired colour is attained.

5/ It is essential to apply the dye uniformly on the wood, thereby avoiding unevenness in

colour when dry.
This kind of dying dries slowly allowing the colour to be evenly distributed, even modified a little (if it is too light, apply a little more or add more dye. If too dark, you can try to lighten it by wiping the dye off which has not yet penetrated with a cloth).
The sole drawback is that the moisture involved usually makes the wood swell. This defect can be avoided by wetting with

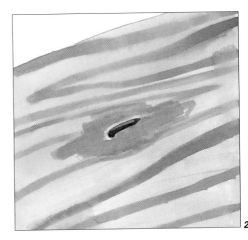

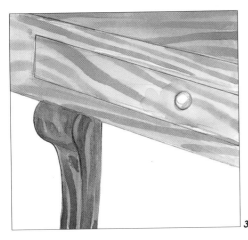

woods, however, will need priming first with tannic or pyrogallic acid. The wood or piece of furniture (as well as the open container full of ammonia) must be hermetically sealed in polythene bags.

2/ The intensity of the results obtained will depend on the concentration of ammonia, the impregnation of tannic acid and the exposure time.
Take care that there are no nails or other metal component on the surface, these will react staining the surrounding wood black.
If needing to examine the piece of furniture during the process, you can make a cut

water beforehand and smoothing down with a good sandpapering prior to dying.

6/ Using dyes with aniline dissolved in alcohol is more complicated as these dry quickly. If they are applied with a brush or sponge, application marks are always left behind.
A spray may give better results but is more difficult to use when not skilled in its use. (The same thing happens with aerosol preparations).

TRANSPARENT PROTECTION FINISHES.

1/ Modern oil–based varnish (also called polyurethane) comes in matte or satin finishes. Its appearance is slightly brownish, it yellows in time and each coat takes roughly six hours to dry.
Water–based varnish (acrylic) is entirely colourless but can be given colour by adding

use lacquer when considering applying a cellulose– based varnish, and to use cellulose when the varnish is going to lacquer–based. Use the right brush when applying varnishes, that is, soft, thick and with a bevelled edge.
2/ Perfect varnishing (water– or oil–based) –something not always of interest when

be left to dry properly before going on to the next stage.
4/ Wrap a piece of wet and dry emery cloth around a block of wood, moisten slightly with water and gently rub the surface to remove any roughness or dust which may have got stuck there.

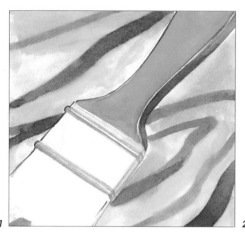

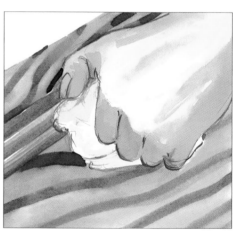

dyes or pigments, and comes in a great variety of gloss or matte finishes.
It is easy to use as it dries quickly (each coat takes around ten minutes to dry).
This varnish can be used as a final finish or applied on top of other kinds of finishes (dyed, painted, etc.), to protect them.
It forms a perfect barrier, impermeable and easily cleaned.
New wood first has to be sealed before applying the varnish: the best way here is to

wishing to age or apply another kind of finish– needs at least three fine, uniform coats. Avoid marks between brush strokes and ensure that the place of work and piece of furniture are free of dust or particles.
Wet the brush and apply the varnish holding the brush almost parallel to the surface.
3/ When there is no varnish left on the brush, lift it off the surface at a right angle (so as not to leave a mark).
Each coat has to be as fine as possible and

5/ Then, immediately wipe over with a clean, dry cotton cloth until all water marks are removed.
6/ Use a cloth for removing dust to get rid of any vestiges of dirt prior to applying the next coat of varnish.

Beech wood accepts all kinds and colours of varnishes and lacquers.

7/ A very pretty finish which improves with age and use is a waxed one. Wax can be applied and rubbed in over many years: each application will revive the finish and give its shine more intensity.

It is, however, prone to tarnishing and is damaged by heat and water. To wax a piece of furniture, this must first be well rubbed down, if it has been oil–dyed, it must be left to dry for a couple of days before beginning the waxing. Wax can be bought already prepared for application (there are coloured waxes available). If you want a particular colour, mix oil paint with beeswax. Melt the wax in a bain Marie, stirring it with a spoon until liquid. Add the colours and mix well. Leave to cool down until it acquires a pasty texture (10 minutes).

Fold a cloth to make a pad and spread the wax evenly over the surface, carefully rubbing it on. The wax mixture can also be spread using a brush. Leave to dry (2 hours).

8/ Remove the excess wax with a rough cloth (sackcloth), and leave to dry for another hour. Polish with a cloth until an intense, transparent shine is attained.

Repeat the whole process a couple of times more and when the colour and depth are sufficient, a fast- drying wax can be applied to make the shine even more intense.

This latter product must be applied on a small area at a time with a pad of clean fine cloth, the excess being wiped off using a cloth which doesn't give off fluff.

This stage is not to bring out a shine, it is simply to remove excess wax.

When the entire piece of furniture is ready, proceed to polishing.

Complicated mouldings and carvings are better treated by applying slow–drying wax (using a toothbrush).

9/ To polish, you can use an electric drill with a very clean mop. Set the machine to its highest speed setting and pass over the surface (crossways movements done light and fast) and end up by going in the direction of the grain.

Finish by removing any marks using a soft cloth (downward motions with respect to the wood's fibre).

10/ On complicated mouldings and carvings, it is better to apply a slow–drying wax (using a toothbrush), taking care to ensure that wax doesn't accumulate in the details and, once hardened, polish with a soft bristle shoe brush.

On turnings, it might well be better to apply the wax (slow–drying) using a strip of cloth impregnated with the product, polishing afterwards with another strip of soft cloth (using shoe buffing motions: from side to side alternating with up and down).

The majority of the problems arising with wax finishes, can be resolved by reviving the affected area using a little turpentine followed by rubbing a little slow–drying wax in. (Leave the solvent on giving it enough time to do its work).

7

8

9

10

Application of the finish brings out the beauty of the beauty of the carving on the handrail of this stairway's bannister, enhancing the wood's grain.

Another transparent natural finish which can also be applied to wood is the cooked linseed oil based one.
It gives a light shine which, with repeated applications will deepen giving a highly pleasing patina.
Put the cooked linseed oil in a glass or porcelain pot and put in a bain Marie until the oil heats up a little *(hot to the touch without burning)*.
Apply with a brush or cotton pad *(always very clean)*, until the wood will not absorb any more. Leave to dry *(this could take several days)*, and repeat the application as many times as needed to really saturate the wood.
Remove excess with clean tissue paper. Finally, rub vigorously with a clean cotton cloth to bring out the shine *(if you want a deeper shine, use a little wax when polishing)*.

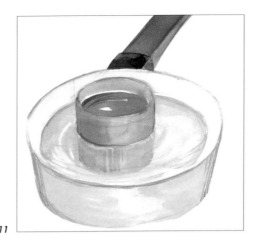

11

12

11/ One variation of this finishing system consists of applying a mixture (20% varnish, 50% linseed oil and 30% turpentine) prepared in a bain Marie, and when hot,

put on using a brush or mop.
The piece of furniture must not be sealed *(otherwise the mixture won't penetrate into the wood)*. It can, however, have been dyed with water– or alcohol–based chemical dyes.
12/ Spread the mixture over the surface and leave it to soak in well for a few moments, then wipe off any excess with a clean cloth. Fold another cloth (soft fabric) into a pad and vigorously rub the surface.
You have to rub until the product appears to have vanished. Leave to dry a couple of days. Each coat has to be applied in a likewise fashion, however, when several have been put on, the amount of varnish in the mixture can be raised slightly.
This is a slow process and needs a great deal of rubbing in, the end result, however, is long lasting and water resistant.

There are opaque finishes done with paints which need protecting so that they are not rubbed off with use, (some restorers prefer a little natural wear to have taken place prior to applying this protective coat on, as this enhances the piece of furniture's antique appearance).
One or two coats of matte or semi–gloss varnish, followed by a final coat of rotten–stone mixed with a little fine oil, wiped off and hand–polished with a cotton cloth.

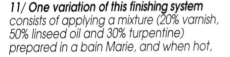

Cooked linseed oil give a quality, highly versatile finish as it can be lightly coloured and gives colour contrasts.
Piece of furniture made by Época.

Lacquer can also be applied using a brush, but this will not give such good results as when applied using a pad in the traditional way *(French polishing)*. Despite being a delicate, labour-intensive finish, it is one of great beauty and prestige, it being the finish used on the very finest antique furniture.

A warm, dry and clean *(dust free)* place is needed when applying this finish where, in addition to doing the work, the piece can be left to dry between coats of varnish.

13/ Moisten some square strips (20x20 cm) of cotton padding with lacquer. Wring out and leave a while to dry. Fold each one in half.

14/ Then fold three times, tuck the corners in and fold the front edges upwards.

The idea being that the part of the padding which will be in contact with the wood's surface is entirely wrinkle-free and can be held firmly by the upper section. T

hese will be the applicators and should be kept in a clean glass container which can be sealed airtight (they will be used as and when needed).

15/ Some of these applicators are put in the centre of a square of fine cotton cloth, making them into polishing pads.

16/ Fold the corners thereby covering the applicator and twisting them a little to hold the polishing pad formed, fold them over to give you something to firmly grip.

17/ When starting to work, or whenever the pad is too dry, open up the packet formed and lightly moisten the cotton padding with lacquer. Press against a piece of wood to squeeze excess lacquer out.

So that it slides more easily over the surface being polished, apply a drop of linseed or mineral oil with the tip of your finger onto the "sole" of the polishing pad.

18/ Apply gentle pressure to the applicator when it is fully loaded with lacquer, increasing pressure as it becomes drier. The aim here is to evenly distribute a fine coat of lacquer over the whole surface. First in the direction of the grain, leaving it to dry, rub down with fine grade wet and dry emery cloth (moistened with a few drops of oil), then carefully cleaned off. Repeat the

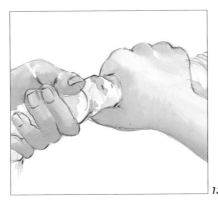

application using a wide circular motion. Several coats are needed to achieve a good seal prior to applying the finish itself.

19/ Use an applicator to make large circles covering the entire surface, using smaller circles on edges and mouldings. Lubricate sparingly with a few drops of oil without flooding the surface.

Change the circular polishing motions for figures of eight, straight strokes of the pad and work the edges the same as the central section so that the finish has the same number of coats all over the piece.

The pad must only be moistened when absolutely necessary, never leaving it static on the finish and always sliding it from the centre outwards. Leave to dry and lightly rub down between coats.

Apply a minimum of three coats but many more can be applied.

20/ For the last coat repeat: large circles, figure of eights and straight lines until the oil has completely gone. On the final burnishing, put a little methyl alcohol on the face of an old applicator (washed) and cover with the cloth, it should be dry and cold to the touch. Polish using a fast circular motion, gradually applying more pressure until all of the oil has vanished and the burnish is soft, glossy and shining. Leave to dry for at least 24 hours.

After several coats have been applied, small defects caused by the uneven distribution of the varnish may appear. To fix these, polish using a block wrapped with the finest grade wet and dry emery cloth lubricated with oil.

TRANSPARENT PROTECTION FINISHES

71

OPAQUE PROTECTIVE FINISHES. Through the years, furniture made of poor quality wood has almost always been painted, it was thought better to cover it with an opaque finish. As and when new dyes and colourings were invented, paints of all hues were obtained and the fashion of painted furniture grew apace. Pastel finishes are characteristic of Louis 16th furniture, though nowadays, many of these pieces are restored based around transparent finishes which allow the wood's natural colouring and grain to be seen. When wishing to finish a piece of furniture using a procedure which makes it appear an antique, a combination of the two finishes is often used, opaque with transparent over it to give it better protection.

On the whole, opaque paints come in three types of finish: gloss, matte and semi–matte or satin. Glosses and satins are marketed as oil–based enamel paints which dry in 14 to 16 hours, drying to a very hard coat. These enamel paints can be diluted (*thin down*) with solvent and have to be used on a suitably prepared base (*they accentuate all of the surface's faults*). Vinyl enamel paints are based on polyacrylic resins (*acrylic enamels*) and can be gloss (*not a very high gloss though*). They are available in gel form to make application easier, dry in 2 to 4 hours and are water soluble. There also exist cellulose–based or acrylic pigmented paints which can be used with air pistols (*or aerosol sprays*). They have to be applied on a paint undercoat. If perfectly applied, the end result is achieved quickly giving a gloss finish, it is, however, rather difficult to achieve a uniform finish, particularly so without a lot of experience and a special chamber, with the added drawback of wasting a lot of paint. Yet more difficult still, is to achieve the right quality and colour to match the finish on the new parts to that of an antique piece of furniture. The simplest course is to buy two or more paint colours already prepared and mix them until the right one is attained. A cheaper alternative is to buy the prime colours in tubes of universal dyes (*yellow, red, black and blue*). These dyes are oil–based but can be used to adjust water– or oil–based coloured paint. Finely ground artist pigments can also be used, but these will need a top coat of varnish or lacquer as protection. Oil paints can also be used in oil–based paints to adjust colours (*but this is an expensive option*) or water colours (*if going to paint on a plaster base*).

paint can be more evenly spread out by going over the same area with the tip of the brush. It may be better to apply a second coat when the first has dried thoroughly.
4/ To avoid drips or runs on the edges, slightly raise the brush just before reaching the edge, ending the stroke carefully.

Sometimes, after painting, the dye, filler or

1/ Proper use of the brush is important when painting: dip the brush into the paint, immersing the bristles until they are one–third covered, half at the very most. Press against the lip of the tin to remove excess paint.
2/ The paint should be thick enough and the brush should be applied bringing all of its bristles into contact with the surface to ensure the paint covers well.
3/ The brush has to form a 90 degree angle, roughly, with the surface. If necessary, the

pattern will come through the paint. This may be due to having used old products. If rather noticeable, the paint must be stripped off the wood and repeat the entire process again. Before deciding on this course of action, try putting another coat of paint on and leaving it to dry. If bubbles form in the paint this is because it has been left to dry exposed to sunlight or an excess of heat. Rub down and apply a coat of lacquer prior to the next coat.

5/ Each furniture type needs to be painted methodically and it is better to follow a certain order. Chairs: turn round (stand on newspapers) and using a small brush, paint all visible parts: legs, spells and the rear of the seat.

6/ Turn around again and paint the back

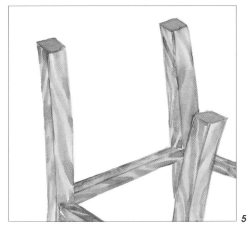

the part of the piece of furniture surrounding it.

9/ When painting a door, proceed in the same way: rub down all the corners so that the additional thickness of the paint on the edges doesn't impede it working as before.
The inside faces of the door are usually painted to around 2.5 cm in all round, a light coat of paint is also applied to the hinges.

10/ On a vertical panel (if it cannot be placed horizontally, start some centimetres from the top with the brush and paint upwards, then, extend the paint downwards properly.

11/ When painting the inside of a piece of furniture, start with the vertical panels (from top to bottom and from the centre outwards).

12/ Next, coat the horizontal surfaces, also from the back to the front. Take care to properly extend any paint which may have dripped from the sides.
Do not allow paint to accumulate in the corners and grooves.

When some varnishes or enamel paints are drying, they produce a whitish or bluish film

surface with the appropriate solvent, leaving it to dry and starting again.
The ideal working temperature of the workplace is around 20ºC.
Bubbles may also appear in the paint if this is not fluid enough or the wrong brush has been used. Leave to dry, rub down until well

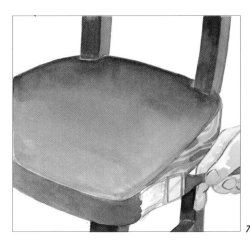

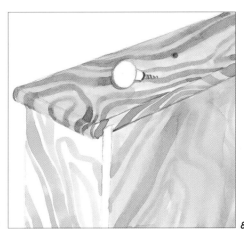

starting at the top and the seat (if it has to be painted).

7/ Moving around the chair, paint the edge of the seat and the tops of the spells.

8/ Drawers are normally made so that the front is lightly varnished. Should you decide to paint it, first remove it and rub down the top and bottom sections, as well as the sides with coarse sandpaper.
Paint the front and a small strip of the sides (removing the handle is recommended), and

(lustreless). This problem can be caused by any one of several factors. The solution, however, is to rub down using wet and dry emery cloth and soap suds, pumice stone or rotten-stone.
Rinse off with water and leave to dry thoroughly before continuing.
The fogging which appears in the lacquer or varnish when it is applied in a too humid environment, or when the previous coat has not fully dried, can be fixed by flooding the

smooth and apply another coat of paint.
When cracking appears (sometimes intentional when ageing the piece of furniture), this can be removed by rubbing down, wiping over with spirits of petroleum and applying another coat.

PREPARATION AND PRIMING. Each kind of finish needs a different preparation, all of them, however, can be summarised as the creation of the smoothest surface possible, particularly in the cases of French polishing and coloured and transparent lacquers. Pores and grooves must be filled, avoid the event of a knot spoiling the colouring of a finish, etc. However, sometimes, in order for a piece of furniture to appear antique *(or those parts of it which have been restored)*, the preparation for the finish could include deteriorating the wood so that the end result gives the desired impression. As always, new wood fitted which has to be varnished must be sealed with lacquer under the cellulose–based varnishes and with cellulose if wishing to varnish with lacquer. For opaque finishes, remove everything that is not going to be painted from the piece of furniture: glasswork, handles, metal fittings, etc. If possible, upholstery work too *(or cover them with plastic sealed down with adhesive tape)*, take out the drawers and place them with the front uppermost for painting. Rub the piece down well first with medium grade then fine sandpaper. Clean the dust off, wipe down clean with solvent and if treating new wood, treat all knots with the appropriate sealer. Apply an oil–based wood primer, diluted with solvent and matching the colour as the paint to be used for the top coat. An aqueous- based paint *(emulsion)* can also be used slightly diluted. Always begin applying each coat on the topmost part of the piece of furniture, then the front, sides and so on. Leave to dry properly, smooth down using fine sandpaper, remove all dust and wipe over with a soft rag moistened with solvent. If wishing to attain a perfect finish, this primer coat can still be sealed with a coat of lacquer diluted to 50% with the solvent recommended by the maker. Smooth down again, remove all dust and wipe down with a solvent or white spirit substitute and continue applying the first undercoat with brush strokes in both directions. Repeat the drying, smoothing down, cleaning, etc. steps as detailed above, and the piece of furniture will now be perfectly prepared for applying the paintwork. A less orthodox procedure, but still one giving good results, consists in applying 5 coats of synthetic plaster to the wood's rubbed down surface *(this is a plastic–based primer plaster which forms a perfect base for gloss paints)*. This may appear somewhat complicated, but each successive coat of plaster takes less time to set and dries as hard as rock. Each coat is smoothed down with very fine grade emery cloth. This preparation is the best one for the application of coloured lacquer.

1/ To prepare old wood, apply filler to the surface *(using a spatula to work into any holes or grooves)*, remove excess filler and leave to dry.
2/ Rub the surface down using a flat–faced block wrapped with coarse sandpaper to remove any unevenness (as opposed to using the sandpaper with direct finger pressure as this may cause grooves in the filler).
3/ Remove all dust and apply a coat of paint to check that the surface is perfectly smooth.

If there should be any point which shows up faults, repeat the process (filling and rubbing down), until ready for decorating.
4/ New wood absorbs paint that is why a primer coat must first be applied before decorating it. It is advisable to rub corners and angles down a bit to give it a more worn, antique–like look.
5/ Use a cotton cloth to apply a little filler in any knots in the wood to seal the resin and natural oils in which may exude later on.

6/ Apply a water–based paint onto the surface. To cover the woodgrain, several coats will have to be applied.
If wishing to give the piece a rustic appearance, mix water with the paint to dilute it which once applied will leave the surface rough and porous.
If the finish is to be of a finer nature, the paint must be fluid, but not diluted.

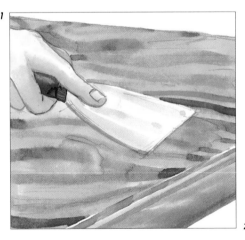

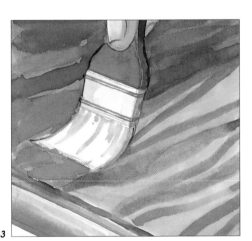

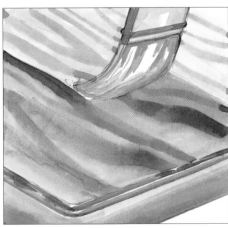

DECORATIVE FINISHES. There are a great number of decorative finishes. The vast majority, though, are the results of variations of some of the basic techniques. We have already covered how to varnish, paint, wax, etc. pieces of furniture or parts of them. There are, however, other ways of achieving highly attractive finishes, similar to those found on some antique furniture and which very often can be attained with relatively little work. A new piece of furniture which has to be installed in the company of older pieces, will fit in better if it is aged or has a finish which corresponds to the epoch and style of the other furniture. Aside from the physical deterioration which can be readily achieved by discretely applying suitable knocks, scratches and holes *(imitating woodworm)* using instruments as simple as hammers, chains and nails; an antique look can be given in this manner to any kind of finish. Nevertheless, any restorer, amateur or otherwise, will logically prefer to base the *AGEING* on a more subtle, delicate application such as giving the piece a soft patina and with some wear on a slightly opaque piece. Pay attention to furniture which is antique painted or with a transparent finish to see where the finish has worn away or dust has accumulated. Chair frames, tabletops and areas around metal fittings, appear lighter because of constant contact. Splits and joins accumulate dirt and are darker. The thickness which has to be given to the ageing treatment will depend on the piece of furniture: thicker goes best with rustic furniture, finer is preferable on more stylised pieces of furniture.

1/ Ageing with wax, use a darker wax.
This can be used on bare wood or paintwork alike. Apply a generous coat with a fine steel wool on the areas which are to appear worn. If wishing to give a lighter effect, apply colourless transparent wax.
For a shaded effect, one or the other can be applied to different parts of the surface.
2/ While the was has not yet been absorbed, rub the areas to appear worn with coarse steel wool: edges, etc.
Repeat the application with fine steel wool and after the wax has penetrated in a couple of minutes, polish with a clean soft cloth.
The wax penetrates the paint and gives it a soft shine.

3/ To age with steel wool and varnish (if the piece of furniture is finished with two coats of different coloured paint), rub the surface until the undercoat appears faintly through.
4/ Then, apply a matte varnish which will protect the surface and give the dull appearance of old paintwork.
Concentrate on rubbing areas normally associated with wear: edges, corners, etc.

Though this piece of furniture has been made recently, the style followed in building the sideboard, and the aged leather of the panels, require an aged finish to bring out all of its charm.

DÉCOUPAGE is the name given to a way of decorating which is as simple as cutting out images printed on paper and sticking them on a surface. Framed pictures, collages can be done, or simply laid out regularly forming friezes, etc. This system can be finished off with hand-painted motifs or combined with gilded backgrounds, gold powder, crackled varnish, etc.

Nowadays, there is a great variety of coloured images available for use: magazines, wrapping paper, books or artistic laminas, reproductions....

5

6

5/ Paint the background for the figures by mixing several colours, ochre, off-white, grey-blue and olive green, for example. These hues go together very well on the surface and readily suggest muddy soil and a pale sky.

6/ Choose the images which form an attractive composition.

Bear the proportions of the figures in mind, and ensure that they correspond to the same style and epoch (if taken from a magazine, ensure that the paper is not too thin and what is printed on the back shows through).

7

8

9

10

11

Carefully cut the images out, turning the image as the scissors advance.

7/ Study the placing of the figures on the background (it is advisable to try out several possibilities before deciding on the definitive one, look to strike a certain balance in the composition without resorting to a symmetry

which is boring to look at).

8/ Apply a generous amount of glue onto the areas where the images are going to be mounted (spread using your finger) and carefully locate the cutouts in place.

9/ Using a damp sponge, gently rub over the whole surface to remove excess glue and ensure that the cutouts are stuck properly onto the surface (likewise their edges), then wipe over with a clean dry cloth.

10/ Using the same paints used before for the background, correct it and add some details, grass, stones, or hint at a pathway or mountains on the horizon. If you don't really feel up to it artistically, simply apply some shading or shadows and then leave to dry.

11/ Thoroughly remove all dust and apply five or six coats of water-based

satin varnish (each one being fully dry before applying the next one). As many coats of varnish have to be applied as is needed to dissimulate the thickness of the cutouts' edges.

Should any of the motifs chosen be too thick to stay flat, one or two of the layers of paper can be removed.

This can be done by wetting the back of the cutout with a sponge wet with a solution of 3 parts water to one vinegar, carefully peeling off as many layers as necessary.

Leave to dry before continuing with the process.

STENCILLING is one of the best techniques for painting motifs, friezes and edgings.
Cut the chosen design out of a firm, preferably waterproof, material.
This stencil can be of cardboard or acetate. Pre–drawn stencils can also be purchased. The secret of good stencilling consists of using a thick paint which dries fast (so that it doesn't work its way under the stencil). The best paints to use are opaque water–based ones or acrylic artist paints. Use just enough paint on each pass to avoid lumps forming, however, should you wish to make the motif visibly stand out, you can apply as many coats as you like.
The paint can be applied with a brush, roller, sponge or cloth alike.
There are brushes especially for this decorative technique: they have short rigid bristles (so they don't pick up too much paint) and glide easily over the stencil's surface.

The finish of the first coat may be lightly mottled, but if gone over again this will be left completely opaque. Do consider the possibility of enriching the patterns by locating the stencil in different positions (upside down, diagonally, filling gaps, etc.) Ensure that the stencil is always kept clean so as not to stain the surface.
To protect the decorated part, apply a coat of varnish (preferably matte or satin). Tinted varnish can be used to tone down the colour a bit.
If the paint has been applied using a spray of some sort, the varnish should also be sprayed on.

12

12/ Whether you've bought the stencil or designed and copied it onto cardboard or acetate (transparent plastic) yourself, the next step is to cut it out using a cutter. To ensure a clean cut on corners, it is probably better to move the sheet rather than the blade. If using an acetate sheet, this can be cut using a pyro–engraving needle which allows more delicate designs to be marked out.

13/ Use adhesive tape to fix the stencil onto the surface to be decorated.
Check to see that it is properly located, lightly dip the brush in the paint, (remove excess on a paper), and gently apply repeatedly.
If using two colours, take special care to keep clean those parts which will be used afterwards.

14/ Thoroughly clean the brush (better yet, use another one) and, without moving the stencil, apply the second colour in those spaces left blank expressly for this purpose. When the colour has been put on, lift the stencil off taking care that the paint doesn't run (to make doubly sure, wait a short while for the paint to dry partially) and if applying a frieze, place the stencil in its next position.

15/ When making a corner or angle, select that part of the pattern which will give the best results there (a relatively small shape or pattern, a square or circular one are ideal for this). This system of applying two colours on the same pattern give a much richer end result and a more authentic antique appearance.
A clean outline is obviously preferable for each element of the pattern.

16/ The stencilling paint can also be applied using a small roller (narrower than the stencil's width).

13

14

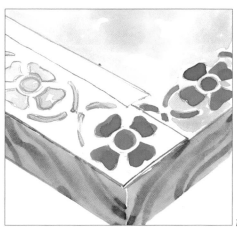

15

16

When applying paint onto the pattern is difficult (the edge is not sharp enough or clean, or locating the stencil properly is difficult), there is an alternative, more creative, method.
Use a stencil as a guide to mark the pattern out directly on the surface with a sharp pointed pencil.
Remove the stencil and use a fine point artist's paintbrush to apply the paint.
The main advantage of this systems lies in being able to mark out the whole pattern in one go (all the different motifs, even those very close together), the different colours can then be applied without having to wait for them to dry to paint the next one.
Care must be taken when applying paint freehand that the motifs are not accidentally touched with the paintbrush.
Stencilling is an ancient art used in just about all civilisations and countries: Egypt, Rome, China, Japan, etc.
This method is not always used to decorate woods, it can also be used to put patterns on fabrics, paper and all kinds of other materials.
It was used to paint skirtings, to write simple words. Justinian I, emperor of the Byzantine Empire and Charlemagne signed state documents with a wooden stencil template. Popular games, like snakes and ladders and the Lottery used stencilled cards or boards and, in the 17th century, wallpaper was decorated using this system.

A rubber stamp can be used for *RELIEF STAMPING* (these can be quite easily found with the desired pattern).
You can, however, carve out your own design on a potato or piece of cork and get a highly attractive result while conveying quite an authentic antique look, which is probably of greater interest when applying a finish of this kind. Simpler motifs work best using this system as the pattern comes out well defined. The amount of paint used is vital here: just enough to highlight the basic attractiveness of the potato stamp's irregular pattern, too much cloaking it altogether. With a little practice, Oriental designs, like those on the lacquers from the Far East or those in the "naif" paintings, can be quite easily achieved. Use water-based paints as these dry faster and mix better.

of dark blue over it using a smaller brush, this will leave the underlying red just showing through in some areas.
Those panels which are going to be relief stamped should be marked off beforehand with adhesive tape.

17

creates a better effect if the horizon is a little different in each panel.
Place a sheet of newspaper over the wet paint and then lift it off (thus removing some of the paint, this finishing trick produces a highly interesting irregular effect and can be used on many different occasions).
Leave to dry.

19/ Meanwhile, plan the design for calculating the number of different motifs which have to be carved on the halved potatoes.
Mark out the motif with a felt tip pen or soft pencil on the cut surface, and then mark out the outline with a knife blade to a depth of around 2.5 cm.
Cut the rest of the potato back so that the motif stands out in relief.

20/ Dry the potato off and apply the paint onto the motif in relief (to get some idea of how much paint to use, practice stamping on a piece of paper).
Place over its definitive location, press down evenly and lift off carefully so as not to

18

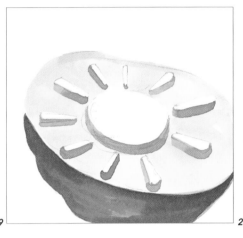

19

20

17/ Used in conjunction with other finishing processes, the end result is even better (the entire piece of furniture isn't going to be relief stamped).
Apply a coat of terracotta red onto the surface, leave to dry and then apply a coat

18/ Paint panels using a mixture of off-white and yellow ochre. For the skyline of the horizon lined with hills which take up roughly the lower third of each panel, dilute three parts of olive green paint with one of water and paint on using a small paintbrush. It

smudge the edges.
Construct the landscape or picture part by part. When having to partially overlap two or more motifs, first wait for the first one to dry before applying the next one, this will avoid the colours running into each other.

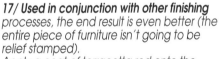

When using relief stamping, always try to use simple lines which can be terminated with some design hand painted with a brush (freehand).
Dining-room suite made by Líneas.

Crackled paintwork and varnish make very attractive finishes and combine perfectly with the procedures detailed on the previous pages. *CRACKLED* finish is in fact an imitation of the craquelure appearance of antique varnish. It can be achieved with both oil- and water-based varnishes alike.

Water-based crackling, a technique developed in France in the 18th century, is simplicity itself to apply: apply one or two coats of transparent crackling-finish varnish onto a painted surface. As it dries cracks appear on the surface. Apply a different coloured coat over this one *(the aim is to achieve a contrast accentuated to a greater or lesser degree depending on the piece of furniture's style, etc.),* leave to dry. The base colour comes through and the cracks are further brought out. Oil-based crackling gives a more pronounced aged effect with the cracks tending to be further apart and differing greatly. Two coats of transparent crackling-finish varnish which form the crackling effect on drying. The finish is rounded off by applying a coat of tinted varnish which is then rubbed in so that only the cracks are filled, making them more noticeable.

Results are more difficult to predict when working with oil-based varnish. The best course is to follow the maker's instructions, use commercial paint for the base and only work on dry surfaces.

21/ Perhaps the best way of getting a striking crackle finish is to use the two kinds of varnish.
First: a dark-coloured oil-based varnish (ageing varnish).
Apply using a soft brush (the thicker the coat, the more cracks, the downside is a longer drying time).
It is better if the base wood isn't new or if it is, apply a sealant to stop the varnish being absorbed completely.

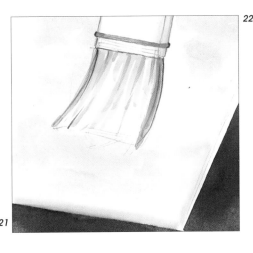

22/ Next, apply a colourless water-based varnish (or crackling-finish varnish) before the first coat of oil-based varnish has finished drying fully.
As they both have different drying times, the top coat will be dry before the one underneath and both will react accordingly and produce cracks.
If the first coat is too wet, it will reject the water-based varnish.

23/ Leave to dry in a warm place to favour cracks appearing.
A drier can be used but care must be taken not to overheat the surface as this could cause scaling in the top coat.
24/ When the surface is fully dry (the oil-based varnish may take quite a time to dry, 6 hours at least), rub over with a cotton cloth spread with an oil colour, use circular motions so that the colour gets right into the cracks, then use another clean cloth to remove the excess while still wet.
To protect the finish, round off with a top coat of oil-based varnish.

GILDING AND METALLISING.
Coating using gold-leaf is yet another of the most decorative finishes, its high price and difficulty in applying, however, almost always make it preferable to gild using metallic paints or waxes containing gold powder *(golden, silvered, cuprous or bronzed).*

25/ To apply them, the simplest method is to mix them in lacquer or rub them over almost dry surfaces. Gold cream is used on red lead (rubbed or painted on).

Dutch metal is a cheap alternative to real gold-leaf, the instruments needed to apply it are a scalpel and burnishing tool.
Graphite powder when added to paints or waxes gives a dark metallic finish, there are metal powders also available in a wide range of colours, these are applied by spreading them over the almost dry surface and rubbing them in, or mixing them with wax and applied in that form.

WORKSHOP AND TOOLS. It is vital to carry out restoration work in a place which is given over to this task. The place should be clean, well–ventilated and be heated to a pleasant temperature *(for the application of some products, the temperature must not be too low or the air too humid).* This work requires space and order. The most ideal setup would be to have a chamber for applying inflammable or dangerous products: strippers, varnishes, solvents, paints, etc., it would also be useful to have a small area set aside for storing saws, veneers and other stuff which could be needed at any moment, and which should obviously be kept as far away as possible from the aforementioned inflammable stuff.

However, it is not always possible to organise such a complete workshop and you'll have to set it up as best you can in whatever space you have available.

It's better to work with natural light, but this doesn't obviate the need to have a good source of artificial lighting installed.

This should be situated over the centre of the workbench or, at the very least, close by.

Also recommendable is a light source throwing light from the side to avoid shadows falling on the job in hand.

Very practical is having a bench or small table close to hand for putting tools down on when using them.

You might also consider the possibility of putting up some shelves or pigeon holes (to hold nails, screws, ironmongery items, etc.) and, in particular, some large panels for hanging up tools in preassigned, easily visible places.

For obvious reasons, as well as for safety, it is better to keep the floor clear of obstacles and sawdust.

The container for putting sweepings in should be put in a corner. In theory, the restorer should not really need a huge range of equipment, in practice, however, work will be made easier and time saved if the restorer does have them.

Such is the case with mechanical tools as well, they can't be used for all jobs, but for specific ones they are unbeatable.

It is better to store them on suitable stands with enough space surrounding them for working in, even for working with large pieces. Highly practical is for each machine to have its own light next to it, the old office angle lamps are ideal for this kind of work as they can be adjusted to just about any position.

Electrical cables have to be properly installed so that accidental cutting and chaffing of them is avoided while working. A catalogue kept to hand should prove an invaluable source of items for building, repairing, restoring and finishing wood, containing more than 4000 items: tools, products and useful materials. Obviously, it just isn't reasonable to expect to start off with your workshop full of everything you need.

There are some things, however, which are required right from outset and then, as more work is done, your newly acquired knowledge will enable you to choose items more suited to what you are doing.

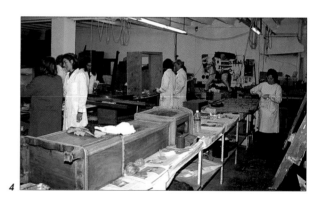

1/ Tools on the walls as well as on the workbench.

2/ Oftentimes, in the workshop, you'll spend time waiting for things to dry: space is needed to get on with other work.

3/ Hammer, file, chisel, etc., all to hand and ready for use.

4/ Large pieces of furniture like this grandfather clock, need a large–surfaced workbench.

5/ Varnishes, solvents and other products on their own bench being prepared.

TOOLS FOR CARVING AND CUTTING. Chisels and gouges have narrow cutting edges and each one is designed with a specific final result in mind. It is better to build up from the basic initial equipment, as and when tools are required for following jobs.

Chisels: have the blade on the end. Chisels come in varying widths and ver often are used with a wooden mallet (when the handle is wood too), or a hammer (if the handle is made of hardened, knock-resistant plastic). Chisels can cut with or across the grain, while gouges and bevel-edged chisels have to be used with greater delicacy.

Bevel-edged chisels have the sides bevelled, the blade is more flexible than the straight chisel and is used for lighter jobs (such as cutting out the slots for dovetail joins if you don't have an electrical cutter).
Not designed to be used with a mallet, but they can be gently tapped to drive them. These tools come in different widths and lengths (for deeper cuts).

Gouges: always have grooved blades, there are two different kinds; one has the bevelled cutting edge on the outside of the tip and are used to give concave shapes, while the other have this cutting edge on the inside and are used for short cuts of a curved crosscut type (the bulging out parts of mouldings), both kinds are used with mallets. There is also a gouge for using by hand (without mallets), ideal for cutting out all kinds of curves.

Cold chisel: though the material used by restorers is wood, at some time or another metal will have to be cut (chain links, metal sheeting or heads of rivets and bolts). This tool is used by hitting it with a heavy hammer. These are essential manual tools and, in fact, you should have them in varying sizes.

Work will be a great deal easier and done faster if electrical tools are used, routers, drills, lathes, etc., with a complete set of varied bits of different sizes and forms.

Cutting tools can be divided into knives and shears, there are however, different designs for each one.

1/ All manual cutting tools: gouges, chisels, etc., always have to be kept sharp.

2/ A small lathe is a highly useful tool indeed. A broken leg or any turned part of the piece of furniture can be more easily reproduced using one.

The most useful knives are those using disposable blades – cutters– of which there are several systems. Disposable blades are pre–sharpened (these must be kept and used with great care).
There is a general purpose knife which has a replaceable blade, while others have a retractable blade which goes back into the handle.
Another kind of knife is the one with a disposable sectioned blade, also retractable and the scalpel with blades which have to be changed manually.
Models of shears are innumerable, those used in a workshop, however, are generally dedicated to cutting sheets of plastic or metal (these require a composite action, like pruning shears with springs), and comfortable plastic handle grips.
If you're left–handed, ensure that the shears can be used by left–handed people.
You may sometimes need shears for cutting out (long or short, straight or curved lines), however, on the whole, this is not a tool which is continually worked with in the workshop, only be used occasionally or whenever having to work with upholstery (for cutting fabrics, there are shears or scissors with teethed blades which cut in zigzag and stop the fabric unravelling so easily).
Another cutting tool which restorers may have to use, is the glasscutter: this is a tool with a hardened steel wheel (or diamond) fitted onto a support. This is used to score a line across the glass which is where the glass will be broken when pressure is applied. The cut can be greatly helped by removing all grease from the glass using a detergent and then lightly oiling the cutting wheel beforehand.

DRILLING TOOLS. Hand drills, wheel braces, etc., absolutely vital years ago, can now be said to have all but disappeared from workshops today. In reality, however, the system used beforehand when working was the same as that used nowadays with a modern electric drill, except for having to turn the drill bits by hand– powered, more–or–less ingenious mechanisms, always working a great deal slower and with less effectiveness than the motor driven one. This is more so the case with modern apparatuses which can also be used at low drill speeds for drilling glass, tiles or porcelain.

With special bits and for small holes, a pump drill and for making holes in wood (for fitting screws, for example), small hand tools such as bit–stocks and auger bits (generally with a T–shaped handle for comfortable handling, when using them, it is recommended they be turned in the same direction). Use a bradawl to start out holes for nails and screws in wood or leather. The main point of a drill, electrical or hand, is to have the right bit for each job, the most important thing, however, is the right choice of equipment. There are several kinds available on the market, these being

to just above 12 mm in diameter). Some have a centring device on their points which gives greater precision without having to mark the centre with a punch. To drill stainless steel or other very hard materials, there are drill bits available with titanium or cobalt tips. For walls or concrete blocks, the tips of these drills is carbide and low drill speeds have to be used, lubricating the drill with water to avoid it overheating. For glass or tile (all kinds of glazed surfaces), a special drill bit is needed. Gloves and protective eyewear is essential when drilling at low speeds. Of great interest for working

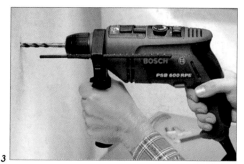

distinguished by the maximum bit size they accept in the chuck (6.35 mm, 9.52 mm and 12.7 mm, for example), for the most common jobs carried out in restoration workshops, the middle size will probably be enough –it accepts the majority of drill bit sizes and accessories that will be generally needed. Variable speed drills are best as this will allow you to drill all kinds of materials and put in and take out screws in press wood, etc. A cordless model may well be more pleasant to use, but has the setback of needing to be recharged, etc. Ensure that the drill has enough cable and has strengthened protection as well as a sealed finger trigger switch to stop dust and foreign objects getting inside. (A good quality drill will be smaller, lighter and easier to use than cheaper models).

Some advice to bear in mind when drilling: mark with a pencil and punch the exact point. Put adhesive tape on the drill bit (if you don't have the special device for setting to the required hole depth). When having to drill right through wood, put another support underneath to stop splintering the piece or damaging the drill bit. First make a pilot hole and then drill through with the selected size, this stops the drill bit sticking and the wood from splintering. Guide accessories can help when drilling has to be done very deep or at an angle.

Two–stage drill bits: to drill wood or metal (at high and low speeds respectively). These come in several sizes (from wire thickness up

with wood are the dual–cut drills. They have a point for perforating and pilot drill, but in addition, they also have a toothed circular blade which cuts through the not overly thick wood, plastic or metal and allow curved or simple pattern shapes to be made.

1/ Precision when drilling wood or metal is possible thanks to the security of the drill fixing system.
2/ Using a hammer–drill makes drilling faster.
3/ Making a hole in the wall is a simple, fast job.
4/ This tool lets you drill with precision any kind of material: wood, metal or plastic.
5/ The two quick–changing chucks of this hammer drill, allow chiselling, drilling and screwing.
6/ A battery–powered drill allows the interchanging of drills or screwdrivers bits very simply without the need for any kind of key, thereby making working more flexible and faster.

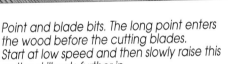

7/ When putting in screws, nothing better than a tool which has it all: depth setting, reversal of direction and magnetic support for holding the screws.
8/ There are drill bits with optimised tips.
9/ A Phillip's screwdriver.
10/ Electronic control to avoid overtightening screws.
11/ A hammer drill, light and easy to handle.
12/ The accumulator block is replaced with the handle clip.

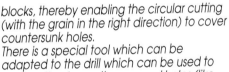

Point and blade bits. The long point enters the wood before the cutting blades. Start at low speed and then slowly raise this as the drill gets further in.
The countersink drill is somewhat more complicated, but not overly so, the adjustable part allows drilling and widening of the hole's mouth (countersunk) in one single operation.
A screw on the upper section is loosened to adjust the depth of each section.
There is also a special bit for cutting plugs or blocks, thereby enabling the circular cutting (with the grain in the right direction) to cover countersunk holes.
There is a special tool which can be adapted to the drill which can be used to make rather larger than normal holes (like those needed for fitting the barrel of a lock). It has a central point surrounded by a circular saw–toothed blade.
Several and varied bits can be inserted into drills to cover a wide variety of jobs (cheese or Phillip's head screwdrivers) to allow the fitting and removal of screws (reversing turn direction according to needs).
Screws with worn or broken heads can also be removed.
First drill a pilot hole using a two–spiral drill bit, then use the extractor with an electric drill turned in reverse until the screw is removed.

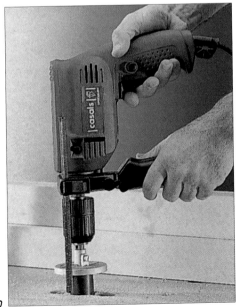

TOOLS FOR HOLDING AND CLAMPING. When you've got a workbench or sturdy stable table, it is highly practical to have a good fixed vise or parallel clamp for holding pieces while working on them. However, besides either one of these two appliances, other fixing or clamping tools will also be needed for holding glued pieces together, etc. There is a wide variety available and they are very practical indeed, though it is probably better to purchase them as and when the need arises (there are so many sizes and systems, C or G) clamps, mitre clamps, cramp frame, resort press, screw or fast adjustment pincers (with the same system used as an adjustable spanner).

It is always better to use wooden blocks between the piece and the tools so as not to leave marks. There are also pincers and clamps which come in many shapes and sizes for different uses in places of differing accessibility: pointed (rounded, toothed, etc.), universal clamps (with a pivoting join which varies the opening of the jaws), carpentry pincers (with curved jaws which are joined in a cutting bevelled edge –designed for removing nails or studs), upholstery pincers which are used for tensioning webbing straps through the frame.
Following, are descriptions of the most commonly used types. Triple screw clamp. This tool has three adjustment screws. Used whenever pressure has to be applied on three points at a time (in two directions)

Resort press. Works the other way round to other clamps, the resort works like a pincer. Carpenter's screw which is permanently fixed to the work bench or table. Sash cramp: is a clamp with two adjustment screws, used for holding pieces while glue is setting.

Tube press, this clamp is also called a bar press and can be used for holding large-sized pieces –like tabletops, etc.- together. If these pieces are irregularly shaped or rounded, some templates have to made out of scrap wood so that the clamps can work on straight sides. Normally bought in pairs and fitted on tubes (of 1.27 cm or 1.905 cm in diameter). Very comfortable to work with but taking up a lot of space in the workshop, are the portable workbenches which have an adjustable which exerts pressure on the piece. Its accessories (bench stops, etc.) make it more versatile as regards clamping. All these tools are normally used for firmly clamping different pieces when gluing them, as well as being useful for the newly initiated restorer as they give quite a few notions as to the best way of

1/ Clamps and screws must always be fitted with a piece of wood between them and the piece to stop damage being done.

2/ A series of clamps assure the pieces and allow fast fitting of screws.
3/ Cramp frames holding tops, allow all pieces to be cut to the same size in one single operation.

simultaneously, like when clamping a moulding onto a corner.
Vise–grip is a clamp which gives good clamping force and which is easily adjusted. It is so designed as to close when the handle is tightened by hand. A lot faster to fit than the more traditional C model. Tenon clamp. This kind of clamp is fitted to the cut wood frames with mitred joins while the adhesive sets. Leaving the join to set before proceeding to glue the next one is the best recommended course.

Can be used to hold parallel or angled shapes (by varying the pressure applied by each screw). C clamps are, perhaps, the most widely used and come in several sizes, from 2.54 cm to 15.24 cm.
As with all metal clamps, the surface of the wood work pieces have to be protected using scrap wood (both above and below). Brace cramp.
This kind of press is vital for gluing furniture and many other jobs. It holds large pieces, like drawers, etc., together.

applying different glues and adhesives. The most commonly used adhesives, easily found in shops, are: clear glue for fullering and caulking cracks in moist places, yellow glues for wood (outdoors), white glues for wood (indoors), and white glues for various uses. When having to glue frequently or working on a large series of pieces, it is important to have a gun when using thermal glues (loaded in rods or specially designed tubes of adhesive expressly for this purpose).

It is important to always use the right glue depending on the results expected from it: exposure outdoors, strength, etc.

4/ These dovetail and mortise and tenon joins form a right angle but, once glued, need to be firmly clamped with presses or cramps to ensure the angle remains right.
5/ The right accessories ensure that a miller turns into a very versatile tool. Here, in the blink of an eye, thanks to the bayonet mounting, the copying bush for template milling, firmly held by the clamps.

6/ Each kind of join needs a different clamp or press. Hence the wide range of this kind of tool found on the market.
New ideas often emerge using different materials for specific tasks.
7/ Any job which requires sawing the wood piece needs it to be held firmly, some clamps mean the piece doesn't have to be moved to the workbench and its fixed vise.
8/ Using a jigsaw and the turntable base plate and the parallel stop (special accessory), mitred cuts (up to 45 degrees) can be easily resolved.

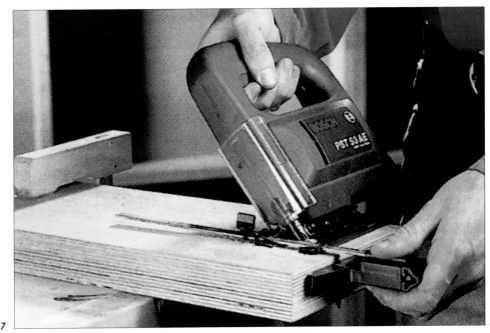

SAWING TOOLS. Handsaws and bow saws, when used for a simple, one–off cut, are more practical than an electrical saw. However, when the workload is much greater, the latter almost becomes a necessity. There are three main kinds of handsaws: the common handsaws, rigid spine *(ribbed)*, and special ones which range from coping saws to bow saws. All of them come in several shapes and sizes according to the job they are designed for or the material to cut. On all of them, the greater the number of teeth per centimetre, the finer the cut will be.

Handsaws are different if wishing to cut panels, with or across the grain. They have to be left to work under their own weight and the forward thrust of the user. Crosscut handsaws can also be used occasionally for cutting with the grain.

A handsaw whose blade has four teeth per cm, is a good choice for general purpose sawing. When starting the cut, make some upward cuts to mark out the line of the cut, this can be helped by placing your thumb next to the blade as a guide.

Take great care when doing this, ensuring

teeth become worn.

The compass saw is used for cutting holes in boards. Replaceable blade saws can be fitted with toothed blades but can only be used for cutting light woods.

Paying out a little more for an electrical saw will enable you to do the same job in less time with less effort, a great many of them are adaptable to the task, this having already been mentioned when speaking of these tools: the circular saw is ideal for cutting wood (straight and fast).

Special saws can be used to cut metal,

1/ A tandem electrical saw (two saw blades which move in opposition to each other).

2/ An electrical coping saw with four-position pendular, inclinable base, electronic speed control with preselection and auto–disconnecting brushes.

3/ Mounting the saw on this bench allows curved cuts to be made with the material above.

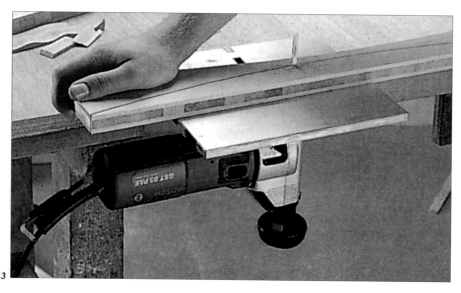

4/ A circular saw should be handled using both hands, displacement speed appropriate to the revolutions selected and in accord with the hardness of the material being cut.

5/ The pendular coping saw is used for making curved cuts in very thick, different quality woods.

that the saw's movements are gentle so that the saw doesn't jump up and cut your thumb. Now continue with longer, more normal cuts (the handsaw at 45º to the wood being cut). Just before finishing the cut, hold the piece being sawn off and move the saw a little slower to stop splintering.

Ribbed saws are mainly used for cutting tenons, joins or mitre cuts (the latter with the aid of the mitre block).

Characterised by getting straight mitres (the rib stops the saw blade from bending).

Bow saws have rather flexible blades (they do tend to break quite easily though if used with force) and are used to copy (cut shapes, curves, etc., in plastic or wood). Coping saws are used to get more pronounced curved shapes in wood and plastic. Essential for cutting and adjusting wood mouldings or inlay work.

There are handsaws (or bow saws) of special bows for cutting metal (the blade has to be tensioned and its teeth are fine). As is the case with wood bow saws, the blades have to be changed when the

plaster and even concrete.

The base of the tool has pivots for adjusting the cut depth and turn to make chamfer cuts. As the disk turns upwards, the upper part of the cut is the side which tends to splinter: mark out the measurements on the opposite side and locate the good side of the piece face down or out from the base when cutting.

When cutting at an angle, measure the angle desired and set to that using the false or combination square (if not too experienced at this, it is better to practice first on scrap wood).

To make long straight cuts, a useful tip is to put a wooden ruler down as a guide (said ruler being held in place by hand pressure), the tool's base will therefore rest firmly up against the ruler and the saw will move smoothly alongside it. The disk's cut angle can also be adjusted via a screw on the back of the saw (remember to re-tighten the screw before using the saw again), this should not, however, project out more than one tooth through the cut piece.

There exists a great range of disks: for fine cuts in veneered woods, with ground and grooved teeth for fine jobs, disks with carbide teeth and special disks for coursed work, metals, etc.

Metals are cut with a fine-toothed coping saw at low speeds. It is advisable to locate a piece of wood underneath prior to starting so as to stop the sheet from vibrating. Metal burrs should be removed afterwards with a file.

Coping saws are flexible but care must be taken not to overstress them as they may break. When making bevelled cuts or through hard sections like knots, move the blade very slowly.

Another very useful tool for furniture makers is the router, the usefulness is described in greater detail on page 40 of this book.

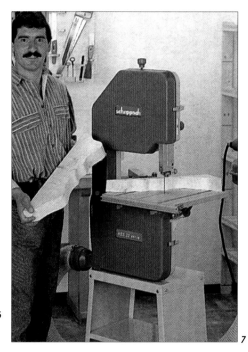

6

8

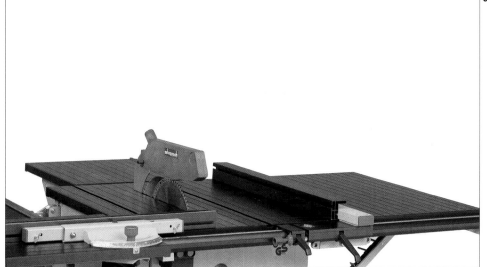

Another highly practical device for the restorer or furniture maker is the coping saw, it is used for making curved cuts with great ease and speed.

This will obviously depend on the power rating of the and the travel of the saw blade. Some models have pivots in the base for making bevelled cuts.

Because each kind of job is done using a different kind of coping saw working at a determined speed, the machine's speed must be variable.

On the whole, high speed, large-toothed or slow, small-toothed coping saws are used. Owing to the blade's action, the saw tends to vibrate, this problem is lessened when the steel base is thicker but the machine has to be held firmly against the piece it is cutting and moved more slowly so that the blade doesn't bend. When the straight cut is started, the leading edge is rested on the working surface and as the cut progresses the entire saw is moved into a horizontal position. Curved cuts are done with a thin coping saw and the tool is moved slowly so as not to bend the blade.

Some models allow the blade to be turned without turning the saw itself.

6/ A high precision bed and circular table meets all the demands of a furniture maker and allows the most complicated pieces to be made with maximum accuracy.
7/ A variable speed bandsaw can cut wood, plastic, spongy materials and non-ferrous metals.

10

9

8/ There are also simpler models, these are robust, powerful and safe, nonetheless. The bench is nickel- plated and the bed guarantees a perfect stability.
9/ Using a pendular coping saw, circles of up to 40 cm in diameter can be made.
10/ Using a pendular coping saw, mitre cuts with an accurate guide can be made thanks to the parallel stop.

HAMMERS AND SCREWDRIVERS. The most useful hammer is the claw hammer which can be used to both put nails in and remove them when they are bent *(when removing them, care must be taken to protect the surface, using a small block of wood put underneath the top of the hammer so that it doesn't damage the surface when levering nails out).* This kind of hammer may vary in weight and size and is chosen in accord with the job to be done or depending on the corpulence and strength of the use. It is advisable for it to have a good finish, should be high carbon steel and have a walnut shaft *(though glass fibre or steel handles are also recommended).*

Depending on the job to be done, there are other kinds of shape and weight hammers: the light or ballpoint hammer which is used for nails and studs, if made of hardened steel, can be used to hit steel tools such as chisels, punches or claw levers (different shaped steel levers) without damage.
The upholsterer's hammer has a small, rounded face so that it can be used in confined spaces (it's magnetised so that the stud or small nail –difficult to hold with your fingers while aiming the hammer at them).

a good drill, has as already been seen, with the right tools screws can be put in and taken out using this electrical tool, but that doesn't mean that screwdrivers are not needed amongst the essential tools of a furniture maker.
Cheese head and Phillip's head screwdrivers are a must, several sizes of each in fact are vital so that the right size should always be used. Generally, these tools come fitted with wood, plastic or rubber handles.

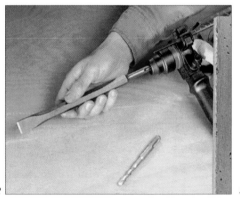

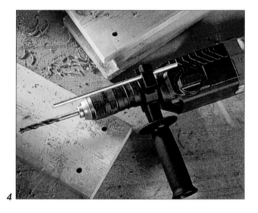

The soft head hammer is used for hammering or shaping special materials which would otherwise be damaged when struck with normal hammers. The head normally has seats on it onto which the different soft heads are threaded. Similar to these are other, also soft-headed hammers –rubber or leather– The carver's mallet is designed for hitting chisels and gouges without damaging their handles while working.
Maintenance of hammers is comprised of keeping the head's surface clean of rubber, glue or rust. Give it a fine filing (so that it doesn't slip when used and may strike off target thereby damaging the surface being worked on), and replace the shaft which, when made of wood, is more fragile.
Choose the shaft with care: it's grain should be straight and uniform. Cut two notches (equally spaced) on the end of the shaft and fit the hammer head over it. Using the corner of another hammer, gently tap until the head is slightly over the shaft. Cut off any protruding shaft flush with the head (at the top, that is).
If you've got some steel wedges, knock these in using another hammer into the

1/ When fitting a series of screws one after the other, preselect the turning force and detaining brake.
2 and 3/ These perforating hammers allow functions to be changed quickly.
4/ Hammer, drill and screwdriver in one.
5/ 4 Kg hammer with quick–change system for hammering, chiselling and drilling.

notches cut beforehand in the top end of the shaft, tap home until they are flush with the hammer head.
If you haven't got any wedges, make some out of hard wood and knock in as above. Lastly, it is advisable to file the wedges down until flush and then varnish all uncovered wood.
As when commenting on the multiple uses of

Those with grooved handles are easier to grip. Prior to using the pistol or battery type, some ingenious mechanisms had been invented to make the job easier: the automatic spiral screwdriver which put screws in very easily by simply pressing down on the handle, while unscrewing it was simply a question of changing a setting on the device and pressing down again without changing your grip.
Also useful are rechargeable battery–powered screwdriver (lighter and easier to handle than the pistol type).
The stubby (for confined spaces) has a short, broad tip and thick handle for aiding hand pressure.
There are screwdrivers with accessories for holding the screws, these are highly practical when space for holding them with your fingers is limited.
There are also screwdrivers for small, inaccessible places, off- centred or elbow–jointed. For really tiny screws there are the jeweller's or watchmaker's screwdrivers. When screwdrivers with worn or broken tips are used, it is very easy for the tip to slip off and damage the surface or the screw heads themselves.

BRUSHES AND ROLLERS. When restoring, a wide variety of brushes is needed which, however much they are cleaned and taken care of –as detailed later on, they will still have to be replaced frequently (*even a slightly dirty or old brush can ruin the results of a finish*). A paint brush is composed of three parts: handle, ferrule and bristles. Boar bristles are the most sought after, horsehair is used to give more volume of a higher quality bristle, ox hair, squirrel and sable fur are also used for artist's paintbrushes. For simpler brushes, vegetable based bristles are used like those taken from the trunks of palm trees and synthetic fibres. Obviously, when the brush is a good quality one, more paint can be taken up and applied better than with a cheap one which would ruin the job by losing bristles. It is advisable when buying brushes to check that they fan out evenly from the ferrule when pressed on a surface, and that the bristles are firmly held in the ferrule. Taking care of brushes and keeping them clean and properly stored is extremely important.

The most important kinds for restorers are:
flat brushes, tampon brushes (for stencilling), and jacketed brushes, a wire brush is also useful.
Cleaning the brushes is the only way of being able to use them more than once. If halting painting for a few hours only, it may be enough to leave them in soak to stop the paint from drying out on the bristles (if this should happen, only a strong solvent will be able to clean them, though the brush will never fully recover thereafter).
Before putting the brush in the liquid, remove excess paint by wiping it over old newspapers.
To remove oil-based paint, put the brush in a container two–thirds full of the appropriate solvent, stir round and press up against the walls of the container to force out any paint left between the bristles.
If the liquid will not absorb any more paint, repeat the operation with clean solvent (if using a water–based paint, use hot water).
Finally, inspect the brush close to its ferrule to see that all the paint has been removed and then wash out with soap and hot water. Rinse out under an abundant stream of water. To totally remove paint, it may be necessary to repeat this process several times.
Finally, shake out and dry using kitchen paper to remove as much moisture as possible and then leave the brush to dry fully, but always well–removed from any heat source. Store brushes with the bristles wrapped in paper (held in place with an elastic band which doesn't grip too tightly so that the bristles are kept flat). It is not advisable to use brushes indiscriminately, but to keep separate those used for oil paints from water paints, and to also keep some for varnishing and lacquering. When storing them in soak, it is very practical to prepare them first by perforating the handle so that they can be threaded onto a rod which can be then put over the container's mouth. It is best to submerge them to within 1 cm of the ferrule.
This will ensure that the do not rest on the bottom and are kept straight. Water, turpentine or solvent can be used for soaking, all depending on the kind of paint used. When the brush has to be used again, remove any excess liquid using a cloth or paper.
Small artist brushes in good conditions are cleaned as per normal brushes and then have a drop of oil applied to them (machine or linseed) on their bristles and are then rubbed gently across the thumb and forefingers, rolling them to give them a point.
Rollers are not widely used by restorers, but when dealing with a large area to paint, it may often be easier to use a roller.
They are made nowadays in a wide range of sizes and the handles can be removed to replace the roller.
Depending on the kind of finish being applied, rollers of different fibre types are used: nylon for gloss finishes using oil–based paints. Felt or velvet for two–component lacquers. Also used for two–component lacquers are smooth rollers for high gloss finishes. The mohair wool roller is for delicate jobs using coloured two–component lacquers or paints. A roller of pressed material is best suited for dyes dissolved in acetone. Small-sized rollers for applying stencils can also be easily found, as well as the corresponding size trays.

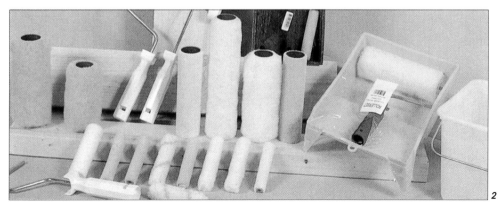

1/ Each kind of brush with its different sizes, thicknesses and bristle qualities, is designed for a different kind of job.
2/ A selection of the rollers and some handles they can be fitted on.

TOOLS FOR RUBBING DOWN, SCRAPING AND FILLING. When the amateur or future restorer comes up against the challenge laid down when restoring a piece of furniture, it is often easy for them to worry more about having all kinds of tools and products without paying much heed to the importance of having a good selection of sandpaper of all kinds and different grades, aside from the other tools which help to get a perfect polish on the different forms. When restoring furniture, very often it is more practical to rub down by hand, but when dealing with a reproduction piece or making a larger part of it, it may be easier and more comfortable to use some kind of electrical sanding tool.

Scrapers are also essential tools and, though they look quite similar, they are not interchangeable with filling spatulas.
A selection of the most necessary will consist of a paint scraper with a rigid blade for removing paint softened by the blowlamp, the filling spatula with a wider, more flexible blade, the putty knife, highly useful for properly applying putty (comes in several different shaped blades for smoothing and giving shape), aside from the spatula for scraping pigments and mixing pastes.
Also frequently used is, a knife for smoothing wood and removing paint or the practical elbow-jointed scrapers with straight- and curved-edge blades for to allow access to the nooks and crannies of complex shapes. When roughing down wood, it may be more practical to have a rough rasp file and a fine one for wood. If wishing to do any carving work (copy a section of moulding or suchlike), a set of rasp files will be needed (small files with special shapes and teeth), however, the best move is to get an electrical sander of which there is a wide choice available today in shops:

large and small sanders, different shapes: band, orbital, eccentric, which, besides sanding can also polish too (using the mop disk, etc.), or the accessories which can be fitted onto an electric drill: abrasive disks, films and strip disks for sanding outlines.

4/ A good selection of scrapers and spatulas for filling, amongst which it is simplicity itself to find the right one for the job.

1/ There are self-adhesive sheets of abrasive paper which can be firmly installed, almost instantly, on the orbital sander.
2/ Old wooden planes are as efficient as the ones made today in steel. As long as the blade is kept sharp and well-positioned.
3/ Today, the abrasive products used, whether machine or manual, are really rather important. The base used can be paper but may be fabric which adapts itself better to the shapes of mouldings and complex sections. A film base is also available for sanders.

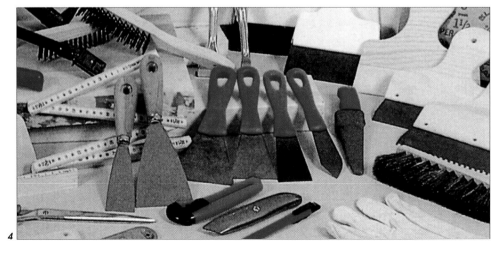

It will also be quite useful to have some kind of hand plane available for smoothing wood (the edges) with more speed. These planes can be metal or wood, but all work in the same way: they have a metal blade which is mounted in a steel base. This blade is adjusted so that the shavings are paper thin. When not properly adjusted and well lined up, the plane sticks or scores the wood (when the groove marks are produced on the edge of the blade this indicates a lining problem which has to be laterally corrected).

When working with a plane, the piece must be firmly held on the workbench or table. Hold the plane with one hand at the front and the other at the back and move forwards smoothly in a broad movement. To ensure that the shavings always come out regular throughout all of the planing movement, apply slightly more pressure at the front when starting and increase the pressure at the rear when finishing the stroke.

5

6

8/ A delta sander smooths angled edges and narrower places and, with its accessories, polishes, shines and reaches right into the most inaccessible nooks and crannies.

7

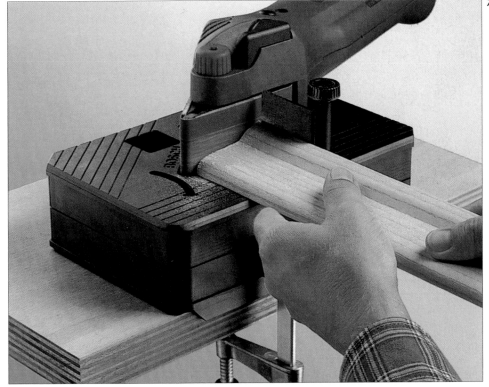

8

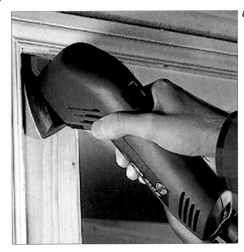

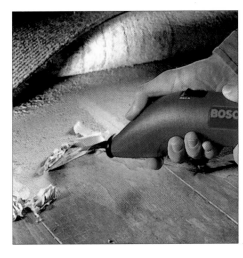

10

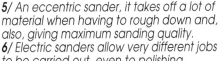

9

5/ An eccentric sander, it takes off a lot of material when having to rough down and, also, giving maximum sanding quality.
6/ Electric sanders allow very different jobs to be carried out, even to polishing surfaces.
7/ A small band sander can sand on both faces, the band can be turned around, it eliminates burrs, etc. Besides being used in stationary mode with the frame and longitudinal stop.

9/ A delta sander reaches all nooks and crannies and absorbs the dust it makes.
10/ An electric sander is capable of eliminating the most resistant residues and can be used to do some carving jobs.

TOOLS FOR MEASURING AND SHARPENING. When you have to measure something, you have to avoid inaccurate instruments *(and rough approximations)*. It's better to use a steel ruler *(mechanic's)*, a folding steel rule or a roll up metric tape. To measure a right angle, you'll have to use a check square or steel square. Metal rulers are very useful given that, besides being used to measure things, it can also be used as a guide for knives when cutting wood veneers, plastic, leather, etc. obviously, when working on large jobs, you'll need the ruler *(or metal tape)* to be capable of measuring two or three metres at least. If the job in hand is small, it may be more manageable and measurements are not so long, but these will still have to be clearly marked and easily legible in centimetres and millimetres.

When building and checking a piece of furniture, the angles and levelling of its different parts are just as important as the lengths. A combination square conjoins many services in one single tool: it adjusts to mark angles from 45° to 90° and has a spirit level incorporated. Sometimes, it also has a trace punch to mark out the cuts. However, if you prefer simpler instruments, a simple shoulder square will do for checking right angles and a false square for copying all the other angles (loosen the wing nut and adjust the arms of the square to meet the sides of the piece's surface, re-tighten the wing nut).

Fit the false square onto the work piece and mark out the profile of the angle. Now all you have to do is to cut following the corresponding angle.

Whetstones are rectangular blocks if artificial abrasive stone (used with oil or water). They

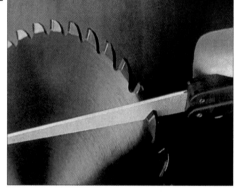

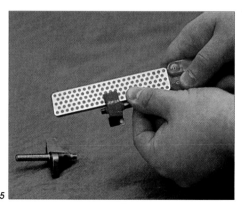

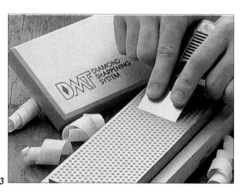

are used to grinding polish the tool, sharpening its cutting edge. They can be found in appropriate hardware shops and come in coarse, medium or fine grades. The most useful ones for the amateur restorer, are those having a combination of medium (on one side) and fine grades on the other. Oil must first be applied prior to every use: a drop of light machine oil is enough. Try to use the whole of the block's surface, thereby equalising wear on its surface and offering a flat surface for the tool being sharpened. If the block has become dulled smooth by an excess of oil, powder or metal particles, scrape the surface clean using a stiff-bristled brush soaked in paraffin oil or kerosene.

To re-level a worn block, sprinkle powdered Carborundum onto a slab of flat glass and rub the block over this until it is taken down to a flat surface again (while rubbing, the block must always be kept moist with water). When you've bought a chisel or are changing the blade of a plane for a new one, a second angle of 30° must be ground on the cutting edge with the aid of the whetstone (they are sold with a first grinding of 25°, but it is better to grind a more acute angle on the edge). Put a drop of oil on the whetstone and rub the blade over it while holding it at the appropriate angle, use an up and down motion over the stone as if drawing a Saint Andrew's cross, all the while keeping a constant pressure applied. When a rough burr is formed on the flat section, turn the blade over and remove it in one single motion, then you can continue sharpening the blade. To check its sharpness, pass the cutting edge (likewise from top to bottom) through a sheet of paper held vertically. The cut paper should show a clean cut.

1/ For carving tools (small-sized jobs with a lot of detail which need small, very sharp tools), sharpening stones are small and not expensive.

2/ Using the flat diamond file saws, bits and tools which, owing to lack of space making use of a whetstone impossible, can be perfectly sharpened, like the teeth of this disk, for example.

3/ The range of possibilities for sharpening with a diamond stone is very great indeed: a plane blade, a split chisel, a worn drill bit, all can be recover their former sharpness with the minimum of material wastage.

4/ To make the job even easier, there is a guide for sharpening plane blades (blades up to 30 cm on a whetstone model which can be mounted onto a bench in the workshop).

5/ Bits of a more complex shape and made of harder materials can also be sharpened quickly and with very little effort.

To check the edge, pass the blade (likewise from top to bottom) through a sheet of paper held vertically.
The cut paper should show a clean cut.
There is a series of diamond sharpeners specially made for cabinetmakers.
The hardest material on Earth is the best abrasive for quickly sharpening all cutting tools (even tungsten carbide (Widia) and HSS).
Compared with conventional abrasives, this new sharpening concept offers a flat stone which stays flat even with continuous use, is easy to use because very little pressure is needed even though the material being sharpened is very hard, is long–lasting because it never wears and loses shape, is clean because the only lubricant used is water and safe because it doesn't generate heat which could damage the tempering of the tools being sharpened as is the case with grinding.

The small circles which are regularly distributed over the plate's surface are without diamond in order to collect the metal particles given off when sharpening the tool.
A mere two minutes is enough to sharpen a tungsten carbide milling tool and, by doing it manually, only enough material just to sharpen a new edge is removed, a lot less than with mechanical sharpening.
Thus, the working life of tools is extended.
This comes in four grades: very coarse, coarse, fine and very fine (depending on the maker, each base colour corresponds to one of the four categories).
Besides the traditional presentation in a box, there are smaller models which come in leather cases, with a clever foldable sleeve which, on being closed, protects the stone or file (flat, conical or half–moon for small tools or those having curved or flat edges).

6/ The photo shows the plane whose removed blade is being sharpened on the diamond stone (very fine grade for precise sharpening).
7/ Besides the traditional ones, today, there is a series of measuring devices which extraordinarily facilitate work, like this inclination compass which exactly determines the leans or horizontality and verticality of any part. It reads off in degrees or percentage and offers a lot of other advantages: acoustic signals, store last reading made, calibration, etc.

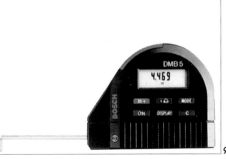

8/ An ultrasonic telemeter measures lengths, but can also measure areas and volumes. It adds up the measured values and effortlessly switches from cm to inches.

9/ Simpler, but no less useful, this precision telemeter (±1 mm), adds the measured values and ranges up to 5 m. It also converts feet and inches to the metric decimal system.

SELECTING WOODS AND VENEERS FOR FURNITURE MAKING. There are five methods used in the main for cutting veneers, as well as achieving different effects starting out from the same wood: rotary cut, tangential cut, radial cut, oblique cut and offset quartered cut.

ROTARY. The log is centred in the lathe and is then turned while holding a perfectly honed cutting blade up against it. The veneer comes away as if it were peeled. The cut follows the layering of the growth rings which gives a very varied grain. This system produces an exceptionally wide veneer.

TANGENTIAL CUT. The half log is fitted with the heart pressing up against the machine's wood and the cut is done parallel to another line, also parallel, passing through the centre of the trunk. The end result here is a well–defined grain.

RADIAL CUT. The cant is mounted on the bench so that the growth rings meet the blade straight on. This produces pieces which vary according to the wood.

OBLIQUE CUT. This cut is generally used for oak veneers (this tree has a kind of curved ray which radiate outwards from the centre of the trunk like wheel spokes). The blade is set at a 15% angle to the cant to avoid the scale or flake figures which these medullar rays give.

OFFSET QUARTERED CUT. This system is a variation of the rotary curt. The areas are mounted off–centre in the lathe. This gives a cut which passes through the growth rings, thus giving highly different appearances to those obtained from the previous systems or by parallel cuts.

YELLOW BIRCH
(Betula alleghaniensis).

Leafy tree originating from the USA. Compact wood, its colour ranging from creamy to light brown with reddish flecks which can sometimes be white. Its grain is defined but not overly so. Highly versatile wood, accepting all finishes favourably (paints or varnishes). Excellent for furniture, panels, wardrobes and other carpentry work. Cuts well using machines and does not easily split when using nails or screws with it, also accepts gluing very well. Can be bought in plank or veneer form.

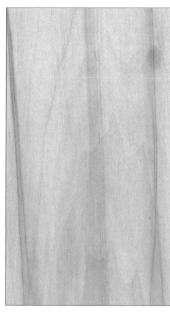

CAROLINA POPLAR
(Populus Deltoides).

Leafy tree from the USA. White creamy coloured wood occasionally spotted with dark stains. The wood's fibre does not normally take a clearly defined position, it is lustrous, however, and can be worked well (mechanically sawn, nailed take screws and gluing), though it does tend to form sawdust balls when rubbed down. Used for furniture parts, panels, etc. Found easily in cut and veneer forms alike. Other varieties: COTTONWOOD, EASTERN POPLAR.

ALDER.
(Alnus Rubra).

Leafy tree from the USA. It has a pleasant pale rosy, almost white colouring, with a not very clearly defined grain. Works very well, allowing mechanical sawing with great facility as well as gluing, nails and screws. Used mainly as cut wood rather than for veneers. Other varieties: RED ALDER, WESTERN ALDER.

SUGAR AND BLACK MAPLE.
(Acer Saccharinum, Acer Nigrum).

Leafy tree from the USA. These two varieties of hard maple are quite similar, duramen wood has a creamy–brownish wood with a reddish tinge with alburnum wood being thin, white with a slightly brown– reddish tint. This is a heavy, strong wood (knock resistant), very rigid too which shrinks noticeably when dried. Used for several carpentry jobs, floors, panels, furniture and veneers too. Accepts dying very well, sawing, screws and gluing, care must be taken, however, when using nails to ensure that the wood doesn't split.

SOFT MAPLE
(Acer Rubum, Acer Saccharinum).

Leafy tree from the USA.
These varieties of maples, like
all soft maples, are very similar
to each other.
They are some 25% softer than
hardwood maples but in fact
have similar qualities and
give similar results.
Excellent for panels, furniture
and wardrobes. Lends itself well
to taking enamel paint finishes
and brownish tones.
Other varieties: RED MAPLE,
SILVER MAPLE.

BELI.
(Paraberlinia Bifoliolata.
Leguminous Fam.).

Coming from Tropical West
Africa.
Light to dark brown colouring
with a strong contrast in the
grain. A very dense wood with
medium texture which is used for
both carpentry and furniture
purposes alike
(flat or offset quartered).
Its colouring and grain imitate
walnut and rosewood.
Accepts finishes and colourings
well.

AFRICAN ROSEWOOD, KEVAZINGO.
(Guibourtia Demeusei,
G. Tessmanni and G. Pellegriniana.
Leguminous Fam.).

Wood coming from West Africa.
Rosy, somewhat reddish hued
with a red–almost violet
coloured grain.
Highly rated for veneers
(planed or offset quarter cut).
Medium to high texture. Thicker
trunks may have a very pretty
pommellé pattern.
Admits all finishes very well
indeed.

Used for making
furniture –both
modern and
classical alike.
Owing to the
trees attaining a
great stature, it is
very easy to get
a large amount
of veneer of the
same quality with
a similar grain.

MAHOGANY or BAYWOOD.
(Swietenia
Macrophylla.
Meliaceae Fam.).

Found in Central
and South
America.
The wood is has a
rosy– brownish
colouring.
Used as sawn wood,
but generally, owing to its
high cost, in flat or rotary cut
veneers. The palms are highly
valued and are normally
combined with the trunk's
veneer. Because of its quality, it
is one of the most highly sought
after red veneers, in addition to
the ease with which it can be
worked and the elegant
results obtained.
Mahogany from Cuba is the
most sought after.

Mainly used for making classical
furniture (English furniture
and other styles),
musical instruments and all kinds
of quality objects.

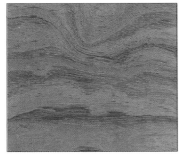

SWEET CHESTNUT
(Castanea Sativa,
Castanea Vesca.
Fagaceae Family).

Of Asian origin but cultivated in
Europe for a long time now. The
colour of this wood ranges from
brown to greeny–brown.
Drying this wood is rather a
delicate matter, but thereafter,
it does work well.
Not very resistant to woodworm
or termites at all.
Accepts dying very well and
gives good finishes, particularly
open–pore or stripped ones.
Veneers are used (quartered,
flat or shaped), and as solid
wood for making quality rustic
furniture.
When in contact with iron
staining can take place owing
to its high tannin content.

AMERICAN BLACK CHERRY.
(Prunus Serotina).

The characteristic grain of this
cherry wood is not as
pronounced or marked as that
of other woods from other leafy
trees, its qualities for finishes,
however, are by far and away
the best for any product it is
used for.
Used for furniture making,
carpentry work and many other
suchlike jobs.
Supplied as sawn wood or in
veneers, works well
(sawn, nailed, screws and
gluing).

CLASSIFICATION OF NOBLE WOODS AND VENEERS

BALD CYPRESS, RED AND YELLOW CYPRESSES and SOUTHERN CYPRESS.
(Taxodium Distichum).

This coniferous is one those which vary the most insofar as colour, weight and durability of its wood are concerned, which in the sapwood is white to pale yellow. The duramen varies in colour from light brown to dark or reddish brown.
The oils in cypress wood make it one of the longest lasting around, highly resistant to rotting. Easy to work (excellent for manual or machine sawing, nails, screws and gluing), and can be easily obtained in either solid or veneer form.

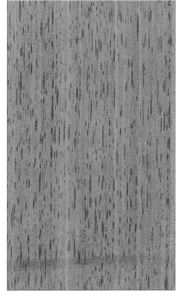

ETIMOE.
(Copaifera Salik ounda or C. Mildbraedi. Leguminous Fam.)

This wood comes from West Africa and has a light brown, tending towards reddish colour. Sometimes, the grain is greyish brown. It is resinous, which makes rubbing down difficult, but the final result is very good. Medium to high texture. It is used for both office and home furniture alike, especially in Spain and Italy (it imitates rosewood very well).
Generally known as ETIMOE, except in Italy where it is called PAPAGAYO or RIO CAMUNI.

WHITE ASH, GREEN ASH and OREGON ASH.
(Fraxinus Americana, Pennsylvanica or Oregona).

These are different varieties of the same tree, the wood, however, is heavy, strong and hard, highly resistant to knocks. Its sapwood is very pale –almost white– colouring in the trunk's heart varies from grey–brown to light brown and the proportion of both colours changes widely from one tree to the next.
Used for furniture panelling as well as curved pieces.
Cuts giving excellent results and accepts nails, screws and gluing well.

ASH.
(Fraxinus Excelsior. Oleaceae Fam.).

Found throughout the whole of Europe, also in the North of Africa and Western Asia. The fresh wood has a rosy hue which disappears when steamed to get veneer turning to a creamy–pale brown colour.
The trunk's heart may have a slight greenish tint. As the tree doesn't grow to large sizes, it is always used for veneering

furniture and other decorative elements or rustic furniture. Admits colourings very well for stripped finishes.

AMERICAN BEECH.
(Fagus Grandifolia).

Very hard wood, resistant and compact. Its duramen is reddish–brown, the sapwood being white, very narrow and straight–grained.
Easy to paint, colour or bleach. Amongst its many uses, it is mainly used for furniture, curved pieces, etc.
Care must be taken when using nails or screws to ensure it doesn't split, it does, however, saw and glue well.

BEECH.
(Fagus Sylvatica. Fagaceae Fam.)

Of light brown colouring but which, nowadays, by means of controlled steaming, gives a much redder brown colour.
The heart usually has light brown area. Used for making furniture, interior decoration, doors, etc., given that it can be worked very well indeed.
Depending on the wood's fibre, the veneer (flat or rotary cut) may have an undulating surface, but after gluing and rubbing down, gives an exceptionally good finish, it also accepts dying well.

IROKO.
(Chlorophora Excelsa, Chlorophora Regia. Moraceae Fam.).

Grows in the tropical zone of Africa, is very good to work with and has a uniform colour. Its resistance to atmospherical conditions, woodworm and termites, makes it widely used in the outdoors but it can also be used for furniture. Its appearance and characteristics enable it to comfortably pass for TEAK (tectona grandis).

MANSONIA.
(Mansonia Altissima).

Grows in the West of Africa and gives a very high quality veneer (planed, quartered or shaped), easy to work with thus giving very good finishes indeed. Normally used as imitation Black Walnut.
There are frequently differences in the colouring on the same veneer and it is not advisable to expose it to direct sunlight as colour loss is occasioned.
When rubbed down, protect mucous membranes and eyes against irritation.
Used for all kinds of office and home furniture.

ANEGRE.
(Aningeria Robusta. A. Altissima. A. Adolfifriederici. A. Pseudoracemosa and Gambeya Lacourtiana).

Grows in Tropical Africa, its wood is creamy to light–brown coloured.
The veneer is cut flat or offset quartered.
Dyes very well, depending on application method used, and may thus lose part of its grain. Finishes are good though sometimes needing a special rubbing down. Widely used for furniture making and carpentry work.
Some trunks give veneers with a highly attractive curly effect.

BLACK WALNUT.
(Juglans Nigra).

This wood unites a series of qualities: cuts well, accepts screws and gluing with ease though it may split when nails are used if not done carefully.
Its weight, hardness and rigidity are moderated and it resists knocks very well. Used in cut wood and veneer form. Its appearance may be plain or highly grained, the colour also varying greatly: light grey-brown to chocolate or dark purplish-brown.

RED ELM, SLIPPERY ELM and BROWN ELM.
(Ulmus Rubra).

This wood is somewhat difficult to get hold of both in solid and veneer form, it is, however, greatly appreciated for furniture making, curved pieces, carpentry work and other fantasy objects. The duramen is reddish-brown to dark brown coloured while the sapwood is narrow and greyish white to light brown at times.
With this contrast, the grain stands out noticeably.
The wood is heavy, hard, resistant and thick-fibred.

AFRICAN PADAUK.
(Pterocarpous Soyauxii and Pterocarpus Osun. Leguminous Fam.).

This wood grows in East Africa and has an attractive deep red, tending towards reddish-brown colour, particularly when exposed to sunlight.
The veneer is plane, meshed or shaped cut. Used in both office and home furniture alike.
Also highly appreciated for marquetry and inlaying work owing to its intense colouring.

97
·····

PITCH PINE, YELLOW PINE and HARD PINE.
(Pinus Palustris, P. Eliottii, P. Echninata and P. Taeda. Pinaceae Fam.).

This conifer comes from North America, and is a hard, heavy, strong and rigid wood. Yellow coloured with reddish–brown streaks. Veneers are plane, shaped or mesh cut. The latter giving wider veneers if done offset quartered. Making the veneers presents some difficulties when approaching the trunk's heart. Widely used as wood for carpentry, doors, solid furniture and decorative work.

Good finishes, easy to cut, glue and resists bad weather well. Sometimes pockets of resin my appear giving a clean or knotty appearance.

WHITE PINE, EASTERN WHITE PINE, NORTHERN WHITE PINE and WESTERN WHITE PINE.
(Pinus spp.).

This wood varies from an almost pure white to pale reddish–brown. It has an interwoven fibre which means that it is classified as having wood characteristics as regards weight, hardness and strength, rigidity and knock resistance, but turning well and having good qualities for bending. Comes in sawn wood and veneer forms. Parts and panels for furniture are made using it and it is very often used for decorative work indoors thanks to its goods qualities for sawing, nailing, using screws and gluing.

OREGON PINE OR BRITISH COLUMBIA PINE.
(Pseudotsuga Menziesi, Syn. Pseudotsuga Taxifolia and Pseudotsuga Douglasii).

This conifer comes from North America, though there are plantations in Great Britain, New Zealand and Australia. The base colour is yellow to ochre, the grain being brown and highly pronounced. Veneer plies are plane or quartered cut. As it mesh is very fine, it is difficult to achieve a shaped cut, the

veneers, however, are almost entirely free of defects and homogenous in colour, though sometimes reddish streaks and resin pockets are present, as in all pinewoods. Works very well and gives excellent finishes. Nowadays, not widely used for furniture making, but it is used for interior or exterior decoration and carpentry in general.

AMERICAN SYCAMORE, BUTTONWOOD and AMERICAN PLANE TREE.
(Platanus Occidentalis).

This wood varies from an almost pure white to pale reddish–brown. It has an interwoven fibre which means that it is classified as having wood characteristics as regards weight, hardness and strength, rigidity and knock resistance, but turning well and having good qualities for bending. Comes in sawn wood and veneer forms.

Parts and panels for furniture are made using it and it is very often used for decorative work indoors thanks to its goods qualities for sawing, nailing, using screws and gluing.

WHITE OAK, CHESTNUT OAK, OVERCAP OAK and SWAMP CHESTNUT OAK.
(Quercus Alba, Quercus Prinus, Quercus Lyrata or Quercus Michauxii. Fagaceae Fam.).

Wood from this North American species may be yellowish–brown or rosy light–brown. The veneer is plane or offset quartered cut to give a branched or meshed appearance. It is one of the most commonly used veneers owing to the beauty of its patterning, quality and ease of working (sawing, nailing, gluing and accepting screws) and good finishes. It is used for all kinds of veneered or rustic furniture (solid, turned, etc.) however, it is also used in carpentry and decorative work. Thanks to the tannin it contains

and the pores of the duramen being impermeable, it is a wood highly valued for making barrels used for fermenting alcoholic beverages.

OAK.
(Quercus Petraea, Quercus Robur. Fagaceae Fam.).

Light brown wood with streaks tending to be green which, as its name suggests, grows throughout all of Europe. It does, however, also grow in Asia minor and the North of Africa. To get the meshed or branched veneer, the trunk is plane cut, offset quartered cut or rotary cut. Consumption of the veneer from this tree has grown to become worldwide thanks to its quality, ease of working and the beauty of its finishes. Used for all kinds of furniture, decorations, parquet floorings, etc. As sawn wood (it has abundant tannin), it is used to make barrels for fermenting alcoholic beverages, turnery work and beautiful rustic furniture.

NORTHERN RED OAK, CHERRYBARK OAK, SHUMARD RED OAK.
(Quercus spp. Quercus Rubra, Quercus Falcata. Fagaceae Fam.).

These leafy trees grows in eastern half of the United States and Canada, forming a numerous group of varieties depending on the soil and climate.
One thing they do have in common, however, is that they are very porous and are thus not usable for cooperage work.
The wood is rosy–brown coloured, cuts easily, does not split when nailed or screwed and glues well. It is easily dyed.
Its veneer (plane cut or offset quartered), meshed or branched, is used for all kinds of

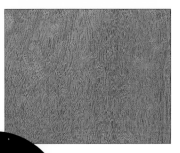

furniture. The cut wood weighs a lot, is rigid, hard and is very knock resistant. Shrinks rather a great deal when drying out and the duramen isn't very rot resistant. Its use, as is the case for all oaks, is very widely spread and highly valued.

SAPELE.
(Entandrophragma Cylindricum. Meliaceae Fam.).

This tree grows in both Eastern and Western Africa and has a pretty reddish–brown colouring, it being one of the most highly valued African redwoods for jobs needing a mahogany coloured finish.
The most highly valued veneer is pommellé, the shaped cut obtained, as well as the mesh one, is done using a plane cut and offset quartered. It combines a series of qualities: uniformity of colour, little porosity, good finishes, works and rubs down very well.

WILLOW.
(Salix spp.).

Willow wood is moderately light and soft, has a high resistance to knocks but is not really suitable for retaining nails despite not splitting easily when they are used in it, likewise for screws. Cuts well and glues marvellously. The colours varies from off-white to a somewhat darkish brown.
Accepts and retains dyes and

other finishes well, but shrinks considerably during drying out and doesn't last well. Better used for furniture, usually used for draws, cages, wooden objects and fantasy articles.

BASSWOOD, LINDEN, AMERICAN WHITE WOOD and AMERICAN LINN.
(Tilia Americana).

This wood iscreamy white coloured, but can be pale brown too.
A compact-structure wood with its fibres being all but indistinguishable. Amongst other uses, it is ideal for cases, wooden objects, fantasy items, mouldings, steps and musical instruments owing to it being a light soft material which can be cut, nailed, screwed and glued very well. Ideal for initiation into the world of woodworking.

AMERICAN TULIPWOOD, YELLOW POPLAR, TULIP TREE, TULIP POPLAR, AMERICAN WHITEWOOD.
(Liriodendron Tulipifera. Magnoliaceae Fam.).

This tree grows in North America but has also been introduced to Europe. Its wood is pale yellow coloured with violet streaks.
The veneer is normally made by plane shaping.
Owing to its uniformity of colour, it is generally dyed for use.
Offers good finishes and rubs down very well, even knots are usually of the same colour.
Does tend to shrink noticeably when drying out, but then tends to be stable.
Its characteristics mean that it works well when sawn, or when nails, screws or glue are used.
When giving it a finish, however, it is better to work using dying by

immersion in particular, accepting paint and enamel paint well too.
Particularly valued and widely used for making home furniture, carpentry work and decoration as well as for musical instruments.

UKOLA – MAKORE.
(Tieghemella Heckelii or Africana, Syn. Mimusops Heckelii, Dumoria Heckelii. Sapotaceae Fam.).

This wood originates from East Africa and is a reddish–brown coloured wood.
The veneer is usually plane or offset quartered cut.
Some trunks with pommellé are lathe turned. It gives a very high quality veneer (frequently curly), not very porous and easily worked. Tints well and gives very good finishes.
Amongst the tropical woods, it is the best for imitating MAHOGANY.
In the rubbing down process, protect against the irritating dust (eyes and mucous membranes).
Used for furniture making for the home and office alike, carpentry and decorative work, giving elegant results.

FINISHES AND THEIR APPLICATION. When studying the different restoration processes, comment has already been made concerning some aspects of the varnishing and the different products which can be used. On these pages, however, you can see in greater detail, what the possibilities for application of the commercial products are. Today, there are commercial products available which can help you to get the best results possible while reducing difficulties of application, all the while allowing a choice of the tone, intensity, shine, etc., of the finish itself.

To get a good finish, it is advisable to limit yourself to applying products of one make only so as to avoid any incompatibility between them, and to use them in accord with one maker's instructions.

In this case, several types of finishes are proposed using products from one single maker (Titán), however, other similar ones can also be used.

With the wood properly prepared it is possible to ensure that varnish exposed to outdoor's weather does not crack or crackle (or at least last longer before doing so). Bluing, tarnishing and cracking of the wood is avoided, paying particular attention to the slits and wooden parts which are crosscut. The appropriate preparatory undercoat can also avoid any subsequent peeling of the varnish as well as attacks of mould or woodworm.

To avoid this, it is advisable to apply a protective coat.

The different types of varnishes have different end purposes and have to be used properly so as to ensure each one fulfils its task, follow the maker's instructions to the letter.

To varnish, ennoble and restore a piece of furniture, a coloured varnish can be used which is suitable for outdoor use. It gives a gloss finish in six colours or can be colourless. Put on with a brush.

A solvent for synthetic varnishes or turpentine can be used to thin or as a cleaner. First, all remains of old resinous varnish coats (patent, cup), particularly if they are fragile, or wax, paraffin, etc., must be removed. Pages 56 to 63 of this book describe in depth how to carry out a proper stripping of old coatings.

The more porous and absorbent the wood, the more the grain will stand out and acquire a darker colouring when given the coloured varnish coat. If, after one single coat, the desired colour is achieved, a further coat of colourless varnish can then be applied.

Another system consists of first applying a coat of colourless varnish followed by the coloured one. To get a darker finish, repeat the coat of coloured varnish again.

Matte or wax finishes can be achieved by using a final top coat of matte– or satin–finish varnish.

In the following illustrations, the different qualities obtained when applying one or two coats of different colours on natural pinewood can be appreciated.

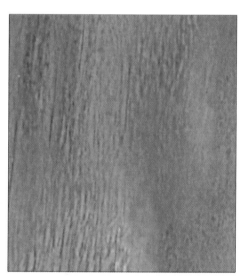

MAHOGANY.
Top, one coat. Bottom, two.

CHERRY.
Top, one coat. Bottom, two.

WALNUT.
Top, one coat. Bottom, two.

OAK.
*From left
to right, one and
two coats.*

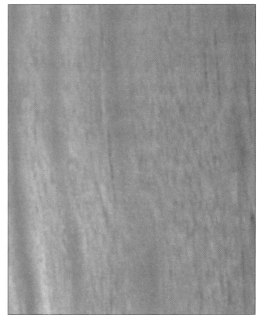

ROSEWOOD.
*From left
to right, one and
two coats.*

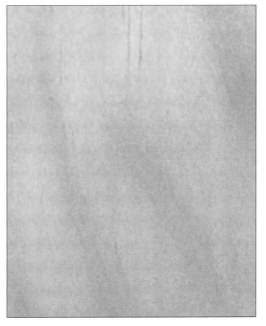

CHESTNUT.
*From left
to right, one and
two coats.*

Always take care to follow the maker's instructions on the containers, thereby ensuring that the varnish is applied properly, penetrates into the wood well, and gives a good "base" for the rest of the varnishing process. The first illustration shows what happens when too thick a varnish coat is applied (undiluted) thus providing a bad preparation. The second illustration shows the penetration of a first coat when this is of the right consistency: penetration and impregnation of the wood is right. It is also important to put the right number of coats on, thereby ensuring that the finish is thick enough. When wishing to get an even greater all-round, more complete protection for a piece of furniture which will eventually be exposed to the outdoors or whose use will make this inadvisable, it may be preferable to apply a more resistant finish.

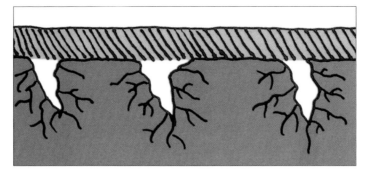

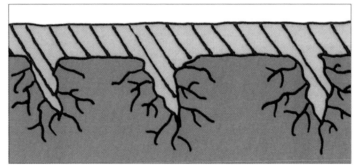

This will be achieved especially if a preparatory coat of primer and then two coats of colour are applied. This product, the result of the maker's most up-to-date technology, constituting the ideal treatment for complete, all-round protection of the wood against moisture, rotting, discolouring, infestation by woodworm and mould.

All of these results are achieved without losing the natural rustic appearance and texture of the piece of furniture. The great nourishing power of this decorative treatment is due to its high content of special resins. The proposed colours are highly transparent, totally solid in light and greatly resistant to the destructive action of

solar radiation (a sun filter has been included in its formula to protect against ultraviolet radiation).
In addition, two or more colours can be mixed to give the desired colour. It does not crack or scale ever because it doesn't form a layer over the surface (it penetrates it instead), furthermore, this quality means that subsequent rubbing down is not needed when wishing to apply a new, maintenance coat. Odourless when dry. Non-toxic to animals or plants, it is advisable, however, not to apply on beehives.
When applying on wood exposed out of doors, it is advisable to not use just the colourless varnish on its own (it wouldn't give such a complete all-round protection).
Made in nine colours named after woods and providing the same result when applied on natural pinewood (two coats of the same colour in each case).
This product is ready for immediate use and does not need to be diluted. Woods to be treated must be clean, dry and free of any remnant of varnish or paint (so that the base coat can penetrate properly).

COLOURLESS.

CHESTNUT.

OAK.

When the wood to be treated is a very resinous one, it must first be cleaned with nitro–cellulose solvent. This base is applied copiously ensuring that more absorbent areas are well–covered. On new wood, it may be advisable to first apply two protective coats. On top of this protective coat, apply two coats of colour (or one of colour, the other colourless if you want a softer colour finish). Maintenance is done by applying a new coat when the bare wood underneath begins to show through owing to the effects of the product's self–controlled wearing off. To apply it on old wood, it is first necessary to thoroughly remove the dried, grayed surface by rubbing down or scraping off until all of the wood's surface is new and in good condition. Despite not containing Pentachlorophenol or Lindane, it is inflammable and must be applied taking all suitable ventilatory precautions to avoid prolonged inhalation, using protective eyewear and respiratory face masks.

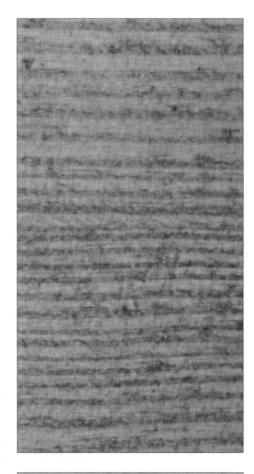

From top to bottom:
WALNUT and MAHOGANY.

Right, top:
ROSEWOOD.

From top to bottom:
TEAK and PINE.

Left, bottom:
EBONY.

ARTISANAL IMITATION OF WOOD. Just as with varnishes, so it is the same for paints, with experience and work, anyone can make the products needed to achieve a good finish. Very often, however, it is just as easy to apply commercially available paints *(proposed by a solvent's maker)*. For example, the special polyurethane lacquer for wood effects can be applied on interiors, furniture, etc, or out of doors. Its colours *(5 shades)* can be mixed with each other to give others. It is applied following the instructions given on the container and using a palette measuring seven or eight centimetres in width. The basic colour range includes Mahogany, Walnut, Oak, Sapele and Ember. It gives a grainy, yet smooth, hardwearing and silky finish. It can be applied onto any non-porous or enamel paint surface: doors, frames, wardrobes, electrical appliances, supports, windows, etc.

Obviously, if dealing with an antique piece of furniture of certain value and which is being restored, it will be much more advisable to rectify and renovate the original finish as authentically as possible, using the same or similar products and procedures as those used in making and finishing the piece. Hence, it is considered of interest to explain the process you need to follow to apply a beautiful grain which will imitate that of several woods. It's useful to first study the characteristics of the grain you're going to imitate *(on another part of the piece of furniture or on a similar piece of wood)*. The result you want to obtain is much more than the mere rough grain of a wall painter.

To embellish furniture, you can use small objects or sections which imitate precious woods, marquetry or reproduce on part of the new section added, the finish applied on the rest of the piece of furniture. In short, art imitates the prodigious whims of nature itself.

Each wood has its own particular characteristics *(as to grain, pores and colour)* as can be seen in the illustrations on pages 94 to 99, showing the different species of woods for furniture *(these can even be used as reference)*. Nevertheless, these models do not have to be slavishly adhered to, the essential point is to keep the general position of knots and follow the rhythm of the grain flowing around them. The flow of the grain arises out of the knots, extending and broadening outwards gradually and gently curving inwards once again towards the next knot.

The first stage is to take care that the brushes to be used in achieving a good result are made ready.

1/ For the wood knots, tie the end of the bristles tightly using a cord (next to the ferrule and down to some 2.5 cm below). Next, cut the brush leaving behind around 3.5 cm. To get a clean cut, use a sharpened blade which is hit using a hammer (resting the brush on a hard surface).

2/ Next, the cut round brush has to be "hollowed" out.
Use a sharp blade to reach down as deeply as possible into the heart of the brush and turn it around. This will cut the bristles out right in the centre (roughly a third of the total).
This task is made easier if you use pliers or pincers to remove the last few "obstinate" bristles.
Now, rest the brush on a top to remove some of the bristles close to the ferrule (the remaining bristles will be uneven in length).

3/ Finally, turn the brush around on a flat surface thereby enabling you to obliquely cut the ends of the remaining groups of bristles and then rub the brush (turning and twisting it) on a piece of wet Carborundum to round off the end of each bristle. If wishing to make different sized knots,

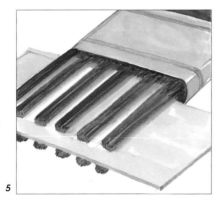

you'll have to prepare several sizes of brushes and round them off in the same way.

4/ To get a convincing wood grain, several plain, hard-bristle brushes have to be used of different widths. Each one of these brushes must be cut to around 2.5 cm in length (as done with the round brushes).
Then, insert a piece of card in the middle of the brush (longitudinally) and cut four or five groups of bristles out next to the ferrule (on the upper edge), using a sharp-pointed blade or small scissors.

5/ Do the same on the other side of the card, remove a similar amount of bristles in groups, alternating with those removed before.
A small, bristle-free, space must be made between each group.

6/ Finally, the remaining bristles have to be finished of as per the rounded brush (irregularly shaped, inclined and the longest tips polished using a wet Carborundum stone).

MAKING THE IMITATION WOOD FINISH. Prior to starting application of the actual painted finish, it is better to first plan a diagram of the pattern to apply and sketch it in pencil on the wood you are going to decorate. The prepared brushes must also be practised with on strong paper, using Indian ink to wet them. It is vitally important that the instrument be the right one as well as how it is wielded *(ideal amount of ink and pressure, plus inclination)*, as this will all help to achieve the desired effect. Several pointed and sable bristle brushes are also needed *(numbers 3 and 6, for example)*, plus a metal comb. The surface has to be prepared as described in those steps for opaque finishes *(page 74 and next)*.

1/ Lightly load the round brush (for knots) *with paint of the colour chosen, rub over a piece of paper until the brush is half dry and then gently push it obliquely over the surface, against the steel comb so that the bristles are extended.*
2/ Next, round off the tips of the bristles by *rubbing them over a piece of paper.*
3/ Take the lightly loaded brush, the one *you have combed the brush and rounded*

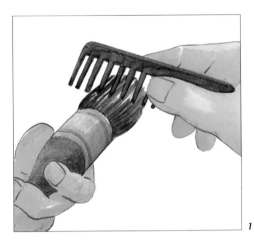

the tips on, and hold vertically over the surface to be painted and rotate while applying light downward pressure.
The figure of a knot with a slightly open centre will be left on the surface.
Repeat these knots at irregular intervals on the surface being treated.
If the surface is extensive, variety in the size of the knots (and thus in the brushes prepared beforehand) will give a much more realistic effect, in turn improving the overall appearance.
4/ To make the rings around the knots, use the flat brush prepared for this (cut into two rows of bristles).
Load the brush carefully, ensuring that there is no excess paint, then press up against the comb to separate the bristles.
5/ Hold the brush well low down (at the ferrule) between your thumb and forefinger and commence the ring on the knot's top part (just slightly separated from it). The top part of the knot is where to start with the brush stroke, this being held at an angle with the palm of your hand facing the surface.
A similar brush stroke is also used for the bottom of the knot.
Ensure that the lines of the grain are sufficiently irregular and that they are spaced further apart the farther they are from the knot itself, also that they join up appropriately with the next knot.
6/ The next step consists of highlighting some lines and knots so that the pattern is more pronounced.
Lightly go over the outer edge or part of it using one of the sable brushes ending in a point (number 3 or 6).
As a rule, lines of the grain thicken and separate at the top or bottom of a knot and come closer together on the sides (they form an oval rather than a circle).
The realism attained on these figures is a question of the painter's skill and intuition when copying the type of grain.
The side of the brush can also be used to make lines

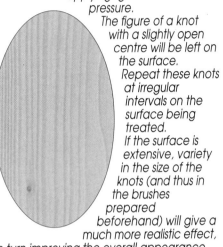

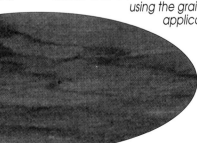

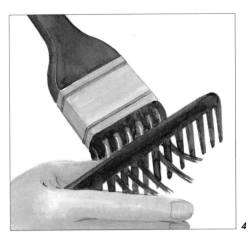

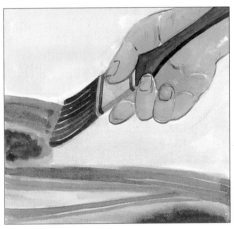

thicker or to blend them in using the grain application brush.

IMITATING MARBLE. The false marble finish is a type of lacquer and is applied over three undercoats of colour which have been rubbed down using fine wet and dry emery cloth moistened with a soapy solution. When matte paint has been used, these base coats have to be protected with two coats of fluid rubber. Between each of the coats, it must be rubbed down with very fine emery cloth so that the result is a perfect satin-smooth finish.

Several tools may be used, but the best advice is to first practice on a piece of white cardboard to find out which give the best results *(it may well be a question of individual preference)*. If you've got an illustration or a piece of marble close to hand, this would be a useful reference and source of inspiration. The instruments or tools which work best are: a hard brush, turkey *(or similar)* feathers, two ox bristle brushes *(of 0.7 and 1.3 cm)*, several squares of cheesecloth, natural sponges *(better if they're not too soft)* or, in place of the sponges pieces of crumpled up newspaper. First, prepare the surface as per the procedure detailed step by step for wood taking opaque finishes *(pages 74 and 75)*. Next, go on to prepare the paint.

1/ Prepare an oil to matte (this will be used to remove the gloss). Mix: one part cooked linseed oil to six parts turpentine or solvent (depending on the paint used).

Then, prepare the marble finish paint: mix one part Japanese paint (of the desired colour) to an equal parts' solution of previously prepared matte oil and mineral oil until a waterlike consistency liquid is obtained. Dilute a similar amount of the same colour chosen for the base coat and paint the surface, first using a little of the matte oil followed immediately by the diluted base coat.

2/ Wet any of the "tools" detailed previously in mineral oil and then apply the marble finish paint while the surface is still wet.

Any or several of the systems given in the following steps can be used, all depending on the individual's preference or whatever is available for use.

3/ Wet two ox bristle brushes, each one with a different colour marble finish paint. Hold at the end of the handles and use both as if they were one single brush. Apply using gentle dabs so that the paints become slightly mixed.

4/ Twist both of the cheesecloth squares, forming a rolled-up tube of sorts then load each rolled up strip with a different colour marble finish paint. Roll them over the surface repeatedly, re-wetting with paint if necessary.

5/ The cut feathers are wet in mineral oil and combed out with a fine-tooth comb. Each one is loaded with a different coloured marble finish paint and use the broadest side to paint the colours on.

6/ Use a brush with the bristles cut into groups (see page 110,

steps 4, 5 and 6), load up each group with a different coloured marble finish paint and then pass over the surface turning around and balancing it on the surface.

7

8

9

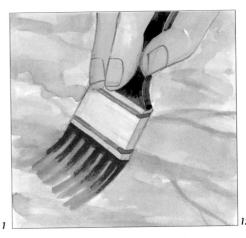

10

11

12

7/ Load several natural sponges with different colours of marble finish paint and then apply by rolling them over the surface.

8/ Take sheets of newspaper, crumple them into balls and once saturated with paint, apply by dabbing them onto the surface or gently dragging them over it.

9/ Each one of these methods produces effects which repeat the most indefinite patterns of marble: they have to be irregular and varied, but it may be the case that some parts do not give a satisfactory result or the surface dries off too quickly. If this should be the case, moisten a clean sponge with turpentine or solvent and carefully squeeze out over the surface.

Take great care not to flood too great an area as the properly done patterns could also be dissolved. Should small pools form, mop up using dry cotton wool. All areas which now look like marble can be left to dry.

10/ The process can be repeated by loading up another instrument, or by trying out another: cut feather, crumpled newspaper sheet, rolled up cheesecloth, etc. Load them up with the marble finish paints and repeat until the whole surface has an authentic marble appearance.

11/ The final touch, is the grain of the more defined lines which repeat the veins of the impurities which marble has in its natural

state. To imitate these, wet a fine brush in mineral oil and then in a pot of dark coloured Japanese paint and, holding the brush so that it barely brushes the surface, paint fine irregular veins on some parts of the surface. This step must be done when the surface is still not fully dry.
The thickness of the brush stroke should also be varied.

12 / When you are satisfied with the marble appearance you've given the decorated surface and the grain effect applied, leave it to dry for several days.
When it is perfectly dry, protect by applying two coats of thinned down gloss varnish.

Imitation marble finishes decorate these tables with inlaid figures.

IMITATION PORPHYRY. This special effect has several variations: granite, splashed, etc., and can be used *(in small amounts)* for ageing, its appearance, however, is still very much like stone. Prepare the surface as has been described on those pages given over to preparing for opaque finishes *(pages 74 and 75).*

1/ Next, apply two coats of a base colour. What generally works best here is to use a grey-beige. To prepare this, mix 6 parts of white matte paint, one part natural shade and one part yellow ochre. After applying this and when it has dried, lightly rub down with very fine sandpaper to remove any possible marks left by the brush.

2/ The paints best suited to this finish (porphyry) are Japanese. When choosing colours, bear in mind that the dominant colour of the splashes has to contrast well with the colour of the base coat applied first, that is, it has to be lighter or darker. If you want a second splash colour (or a third even), these should also contrast with the base colour too. For instance: grey-beige base colour (pale), splashed with dark brown and a light, brighter than the base, beige.

The colours can be as varied as they are in the reality seen on stones in nature.

3/ For each one of the splash colours, mix up one part of Japanese paint to three of pure turpentine and one tenth part of the same volume of Japanese drier.
Wet a short, thick-bristled flat brush halfway up the bristles in the first splash colour. Bang the brush's ferrule against a block of wood held in the air while moving the brush over the surface (without touching it). This will release large drops of paint (it is highly advisable to try this out first on a piece of white cardboard until sufficiently skilled in the technique, ie, amount of paint, intensity of knocks, brush movement speed, etc.) To use another colour with the brush, this must be thoroughly cleaned using the appropriate solvent.

4/ To make the second application (with finer drops), slowly run the tip of your forefinger (suitably protected with rubber gloves) over the edge of the brush's bristles.
This will produce a uniform showering of paint droplets over the surface.
If the desired effect is thus obtained, this may be enough, however, another fine shower can be applied, if so desired, using a completely different colour like yellow or red.

5/ If a large paint drip should accidentally happen, or splashing be done which is not intentional, it is best to remove it when it has dried, scraping it off with a razor blade or sharp knife.
This operation must be done very carefully so as not to damage the base coat.
Once removed, the area can be treated again.

6/ The final touch (optional), could be to apply a fine shower of gold which is applied as per step 4 on this page.
The gold is prepared with a quarter part of brilliant gold metalflake, one part gilding sisal and a quarter part of pure turpentine.
Black or white drops can also be added to attain the desired finish.
The final finish will always be protected by two coats of transparent varnish (which can be further perfected by fine hand-polishing and coat of wax furniture polish which is then rubbed until a soft sheen is achieved).

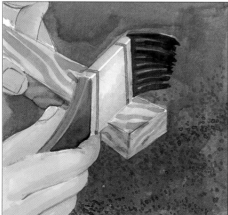

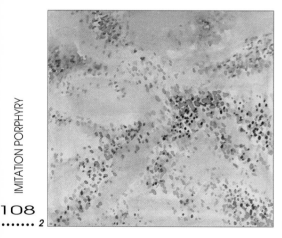

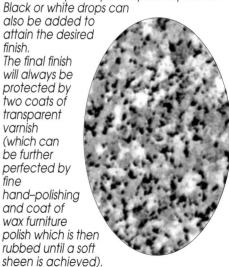

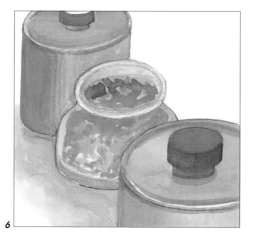

IMITATION CAREY. When wishing to apply a reasonably convincing Carey finish, the first step is to think of is that the surface must be flat or slightly convex and not too large because the shell sheets of this turtle can never be larger than 15 cm on a side, and do not admit accentuated carvings or reliefs. *(If all you want is a fantasy finish, this doesn't have to be considered).* When the imitation finish is done to replace the loss of an authentic piece of Carey, the model to follow will always be the intact part of the shell, always endeavouring to match up with its colour and texture. Care must be taken to mask the surrounding Carey off with rubber putty so that the paint applied doesn't come into contact with it. When this is dry, remove the masking by rubbing off with your fingers and then polish the Carey with a paste made using cassia powder and olive oil.

1/ The background colour is somewhere between ivory and pale yellow. To obtain this, mix the following ingredients: eight parts white matte paint, half volume of yellow ochre Japanese pigment and one part yellow chrome Japanese pigment. When needing to match up exactly with a piece of Carey, these proportions can be varied slightly to get the required colour match. Apply three coats, rubbing down between each coat with emery cloth wet in a soapy water mixture. When the last coat has dried, protect with a coat of thinned white rubber lacquer and, once the surface has dried, trace out the marks on the background colour using a sharp pencil.

2/ These marks appear to radiate out from a central point. The first transparent brushstrokes of the scored pattern of the turtle's shell are applied using a 2.5 cm ox bristle brush or with a makeup sponge. Cover just over half of the background with a bath of : asphalt, Japanese drier and hot undiluted outdoors varnish, add two parts solvent to this mixture.

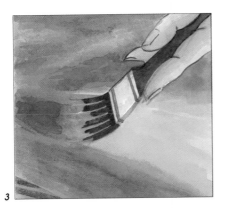

3/ When this has dried, protect by applying diluted rubber lacquer. The following marks are always applied using small radial brushstrokes in the same way as before. First, rub the surface with matte oil (page 106, step 1), and apply a mixture of yellow ochre pigment and natural sienna diluted in equal parts with transparent varnish to which a pinch of Japanese drier has been added. Apply using a 1.3 cm brush covering approximately half of the surface (separating the radial

brushstrokes), brushstrokes must be varied: thin, thick, short, long and always at irregular intervals.
4/ After this application of yellow ochre and prior to it drying, the edges of each brushstroke have to be blurred out using a piece of cotton. This slight touching up of brushstrokes makes them translucid and the blurred edges seem more like authentic Carey. When dry, this first application has to be protected with a coat of diluted rubber lacquer.
5/ A second, third and fourth application of these marks is done in the same way, over or next to the previous ones. To apply these coats, use the formula given in step 3, but here using oil colours: natural sienna, natural shadow and toasted shadow. After each application, blur the brushstrokes (as described in step 4), and then seal with a coat of rubber lacquer. Avoid marks which are too regular or parallel and ensure that brushstrokes are as varied as possible.
6/ Finally, apply some highlights in the form of tiny rhomboids using the following mixture: one part Japanese toasted shadow pigment to one quarter part of lampblack. A number 6 artist's paintbrush has to be used to apply the highlights in isolation or groups, applying them at a slight angle to the existing brushstrokes. Protect with two coats of diluted rubber lacquer. Rub down with very fine emery cloth wet in soapy water between coats. After the final treatment, carefully wash the imitation Carey.

Glass display cabinet.

Whether wishing to build a piece of furniture itself or just restore one, it is essential to have a clear idea of all the component parts comprising it and the technique required for their proper assembly. The drawing of this project - displaying a great many characteristics of the Queen Anne English style- the whole piece of furniture and its main parts can be seen of this magnificent glass display cabinet.

It is made out of pine finished in walnut colouring and varnished. The lower section is comprised of a double-doored cupboard with a shelf dividing up the space inside, plus two drawers under the top on which the glass display cabinet rests, this forming the top part of the piece of furniture.

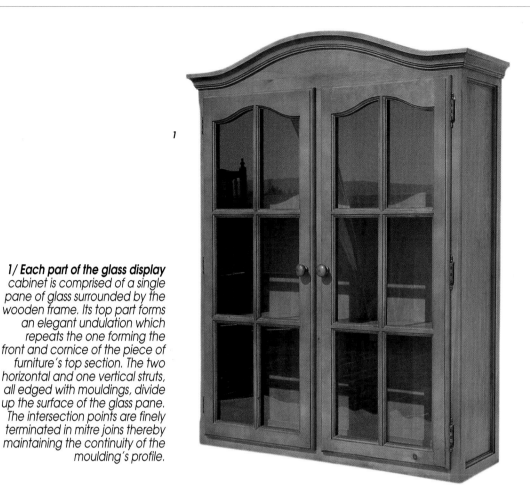

1/ Each part of the glass display cabinet is comprised of a single pane of glass surrounded by the wooden frame. Its top part forms an elegant undulation which repeats the one forming the front and cornice of the piece of furniture's top section. The two horizontal and one vertical struts, all edged with mouldings, divide up the surface of the glass pane. The intersection points are finely terminated in mitre joins thereby maintaining the continuity of the moulding's profile.

4/ The balanced proportions and the perfection of the details, are some of the most outstanding qualities to be attained by the furniture maker.

This illustration also shows the mouldings of the top cornice and the skirting around the base is extended around the sides. This type of projected moulding are always superimposed on the structure as is the case here. The top part of the glass display cabinet is made out of plywood.

3/ The lines of distribution of the diverse spaces are absolute regular. Thus, in the lower part of the piece of furniture, the width of the drawers coincides with that of the doors, and the perimeter of the different elements is formed by a simple moulding. Obviously, the doors are bigger and their structure is based around a frame with an interior panel. The front of each drawer is formed out of a single piece of solid wood, broken up solely by the handle.

2/ The structure of the lower section is based around struts and beams of straight lines joined by mortise and tenon joins, gentle mouldings of concave curves flanked by parallel lines for the cornice of the top and, similarly decorated, those forming the low-height plinth on which this structure rests. The top parts of the door frames have an crossbow-shaped wave which is repeated on the top part of the piece of furniture.

GLASS DISPLAY CABINET

111
....

5

6

7

5/ View of one of the top corners of the front part, showing the finish of the piece of furniture's top section with the moulding which also serves as a cornice (its corner cut in mitre). Contrariwise, it can be clearly seen that the door frame is joined with a half join leaving the vertical struts on the end of the horizontal pieces visible.
The brass hinge is finished in old gold. There are three fitted to each door of the glass display cabinet. The frame's rounded shape helps its insertion and working.

6/ This photograph shows the left hand bottom corner of the piece of furniture. It perfectly shows the structure of the base with mouldings and sphere-shaped legs adorned with a fine horizontal ring which gently delineates its equator.

7/ The elegance of the simple shapes is reflected in the simple door and drawer handles. They are made out of wood turned in a slightly oblate ball shape, fitted onto a cylindrical base (like a ring), which is applied directly onto the wood of the frame by using an appropriate screw.
All of the handles are the same size.

11

11/ View showing the triangular piece used to brace the fixing of the top cornice on each corner. The finish of pieces of furniture, even those of high quality, is generally limited to the wood areas left visible. Hence, it is better to thoroughly inspect them on a regular basis, paying particular attention to the untreated wood pieces. The possibility of an infection by woodworm always exists, this will be much easier to treat and eradicate if caught at an early stage.

8/ The rear of the lower section of the piece of furniture, is formed by the corresponding frame of the structure and the panel enclosing the back of the piece of furniture is made out of hard cardboard. This is a material which, owing to its strength and elasticity, stands up well to all the changes in the wood, without deforming or damaging the structural joins. Wood is a "live" material which dilates with changes in humidity, etc. It is well known that the greatest danger to solid wood furniture consists in the deformations and stresses suffered by them in their different parts, particularly so when the direction of the wood fibres do not coincide, the result being cracks, splits, etc. The hanging metal piece is what braces and protects the join between the top and bottom of the piece of furniture on this side. Obviously, this fixing is repeated on the other side too, thereby fully securing the glass display cabinet onto the lower section of the piece of furniture.

9/ This photograph shows the frontal extension of the cornice crowning the piece of furniture. It is gently curved, rising in the centre and is underscored by the pattern of the triple moulding. This same design, on a smaller scale, is repeated on the inside of the door frames and the side struts of the piece of furniture. In each case they frame both the glass panes and the corresponding panels. Both are fitted by inserting them in their appropriate groove.

10/ This photograph shows the image of one of the drawers seen in profile, perfectly displaying its construction with dovetail joins and front with the rounded edge. The bottom of the drawers is made out of plywood which is fixed by means of slotting into the relevant groove inset all around the drawer.
When making pieces of furniture, for a long time now, care has been taken to use techniques which avoid as much as possible the use of metal nails and screws. This is the reason behind the different kinds of joins and assemblies of the different pieces. All of the joins contribute to the solidness and indefinite duration of the piece of furniture, further enhanced if a good quality adhesive is used.

12/ When making a piece of furniture, it is essential to properly choose the woods for each one of the component parts, as well as the direction of their fibres, particularly so when the pieces of wood are used on the piece's exterior. This photograph shows the vertical grain of the side panel contrasting with the horizontal one of the drawer fronts. This remains visible even after a slight tinting of walnut colouring and varnish.

Bed. The actual concept of the comfort desired for a bed has varied considerably throughout the ages: in the Middle Ages, beds seemed more like wardrobes than actual beds, back then it was inconceivable to think of a bed without its corresponding canopy. These gradually changed through various shapes and sizes. The best kind of bed was considered as being soft, this being achieved by putting in more mattresses and increasing their thickness until a small step or even ladder was required to get into bed, (the height and luxury of the hangings were also signs of the status of the user and the solemnity they were trying to achieve with their bed). Remember that kings and nobility held audiences when they were resting or having just awakened. The steel spring mattress was one of the modern inventions which proved groundless the myth that the thicker the mattress the more comfortable it was, but the still prevalent belief was that a soft bed was better.

It is more than proven today that a certain rigidity improves comfort and aids sleep. Wooden laminas provide elasticity, and a good mattress has more rigid points to ensure that the spine rests in the right position.

In short: a bed today is completely different to an antique one, nevertheless, the head and foot boards still continue to reproduce the lines from all styles.

The bed whose construction we are looking at here is reminiscent of the Chippendale pieces of furniture bearing a Chinese influence and its turned bars correspond to the Baroque style of Spain and Portugal. One of the advantages of building a piece of furniture consists of the fact that, whatever style you choose the dimensions can be modernised.

This, then, removes the difficulty of having to have the bed's base or mattress made especially to size.

Nowadays, there is a tendency to beds being somewhat longer than of old (the average height has increased in this century), and the widths have been unified within set parameters, this means that replacing or renovating a mattress or bed base is problem free.

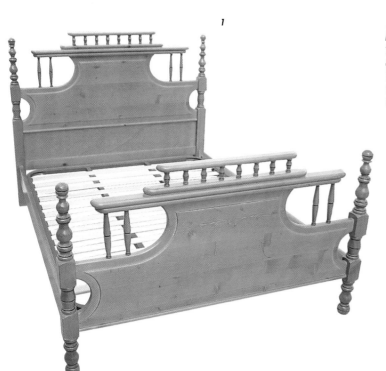

1/ This photograph shows a solid, honey-coloured, pinewood bed the construction of which is commented on in these pages. To simplify the construction of the panels used as head and foot boards, they are both the same and the greater height of the headboard is achieved by adding a plain, rectangular panel underneath the one giving the piece the original design.

4/ The topmost point of the headboard is done with a rectangle added underneath the designed piece, the height of the legs which form two turned columns at the top, however, is also greater. Contrariwise, the lower part of them is unworked and is rectangular sectioned all the way down to the floor.

2/ This frontal view shows the legs of the bed, the construction of this part can be appreciated here: two large ball-turned columns, rings and balustrades used as legs and with two parallelepiped-shaped sections on which it is easier to make the connection of the side ends of the main soffit. Actually the same design, finished in two projections separated by a curve (almost a semi-circumference) gives the projection (or spigot) with the ideal design for fitting into the mortise cut into flat side of said part of the turned bar.

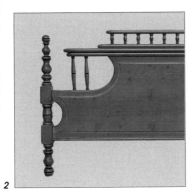

On the soffit which, on the legs has the central outside part in relief (continuing the same pattern as its silhouette), there is cornice of sorts with two split canes (convex) and separated from the third, lesser-sized one. On the ledge of sorts formed by this frieze (which has the same relief on the two sides), there is a series of eight turned columns inserted which bear the top finial of this part of the bed: a rounded edged piece of wood which forms a kind of top rail.

3/ The top part of the headboard and the legs of the bed have the same design and are made with the same measurements.

5/ This view shows the panel's finial which, as can be seen is the result of a triple moulding and is composed of two boards (slightly longer than the upper one), with rounded edges on which another, narrower shorter one, has been fitted which gives support to the columns of the top finial.

6/ This photograph shows in great detail the fitting of the headboard and beam: two pins and the typical cutting which is used for introducing the pin which will firmly hold the two pieces in place.
As almost always happens, the finish of the headboard is different from the plainer one on the inside of the beam.

7/ This other view of the join between the beam and legs of the bed, the pin is in place and ready to be adjusted.

11/ The columns which correspond to the legs of the beds are turned and decorated down to floor level. The end is formed by a ball with two horizontal lines which are highlighted in a dark tone.

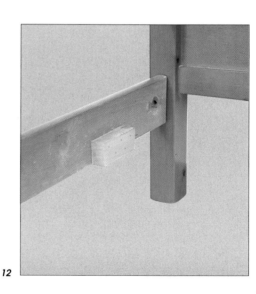

12/ The important thing ensuring that a bed is stable, consists in the correct position of the beams (properly squared up) with the headboard and legs, as well as the solid assembly of the parts used to support the base and the legs being levelled

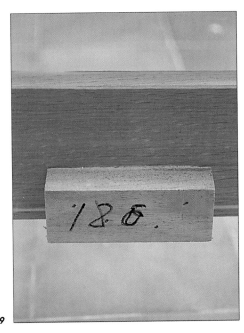

8/ The grooves and rings of the turned pieces are highlighted by a dark line which is used to better bring out the workmanship of said pieces. On older pieces of furniture, the turning was yet another point in favour of the cabinetmaker.

As turning machinery has improved over the years, it being possible nowadays to make exact copies of any part, pieces with this decoration have been relegated to rustic pieces of furniture. They do, however, have a highly decorative effect which enriches the design.

9/ The photograph shows the perfect fit of the beam and headboard.
The finish on the outside of the bed's side is the same as that on the rest of the piece of furniture.
Light-coloured pieces of furniture with transparent finishes are no more delicate than darker ones because the varnishes of today protect the wood and are very tough. If wishing to get a less glossy shine, a little wax should be applied and rubbed in with a soft cloth.

10/ This piece of wood firmly pinned onto the beam, besides giving the bed base the proper length, is also used to support it together with the others so fitted that, simply placed on top of them, they cannot move wherever weight is applied on them (by the user sitting or laying down).

13/ The different pieces which comprise the boards of the head and foot boards, are tongue and grooved. The parts which are inserted in the columns forming the four corners are done using mortise and tenon.

Bedside table. The charm, a little naive perhaps, of a rustic style piece of furniture, perfectly combines with current tastes for simple clean lines. If the fact that they are made out of selected solid Spanish pine woods is added in too, the result is a timeless piece of furniture with a discrete beauty and elegance which can rub shoulders with other, more valuable, pieces (antiques) to make up the furniture of any bedroom. If only antiques are used to furnish a room it has the appearance of a museum setting.
 It is much more satisfying to harmoniously combine furniture from different styles and epochs which have something in common.
In this case, that nexus could very well be solid wood and the rustic style (Provençal). This bedside table is not antique nor does it try to be, quite the opposite in fact. The following comments will highlight construction details which may be of help to the amateur (with a certain level of experience in carpentry) in making the same or similar piece of furniture.

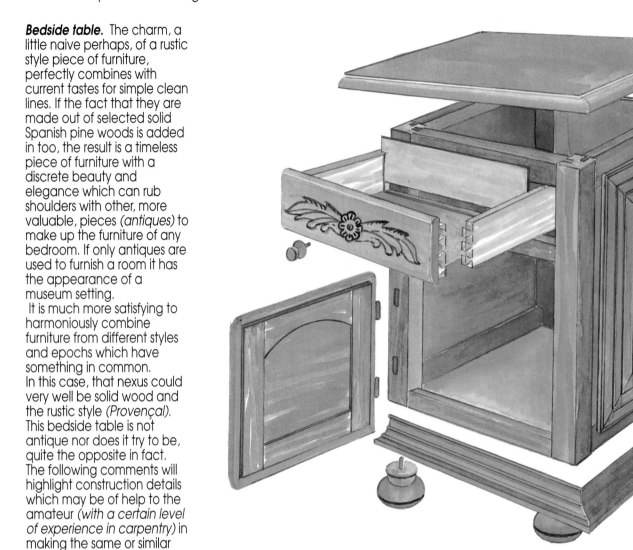

1

2

1/ This foreshortened view of the piece of furniture, principally shows the front of the drawer which is decorated with the pattern of an eight-petaled flower and flanked by two symmetrical leaves.
It isn't a naturalist type pattern and is deeply engraved in the wood. The finish highlights the outlines in a dark tone.
In the foreground, the top of the bedside table can be seen with the moulded edging.
The varnishing brings out the beauty of the wood and its iridescence.

2/ This photograph perfectly shows the structure: thick strips on the corners which are scarf-joined with those corresponding to the top part, the base and which separate the part appertaining to the drawer which forms the cupboard section. In the opening, the pieces of wood forming the guides can be seen, along which the drawer moves in and out. The beauty of the grain on the moulding stands out (ovaled) which forms the edges of the top.

3/ This piece of furniture
has a honey-coloured finish which allows the wood grain to stand out, it has been thought better to leave a knot or two visible (highlighting further the simplicity and rusticity of the piece). The finish has a soft sheen and gives protection as well as enhancing the bedside table. The distribution is the traditional one for this kind of furniture: a drawer under the top and cupboard underneath.

3

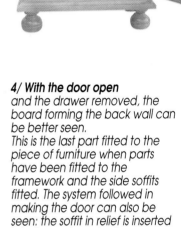

4

4/ With the door open
and the drawer removed, the board forming the back wall can be better seen.
This is the last part fitted to the piece of furniture when parts have been fitted to the framework and the side soffits fitted. The system followed in making the door can also be seen: the soffit in relief is inserted into the rectangular frame. The top part of said soffit is slightly arched.

5

5/ The front legs are turned and
rest on the floor on large ball feet with a horizontal line striating them (like a yoyo). Both are one-piece units and have other turnings and rings, but always of lesser diameter than the base.
They are fitted close to the corners, onto a bracket on the framework so as not to weaken the joins of the corners of the structure's lower part.

6

6/ The second part of the closure
is, obviously, installed on the edge of the doorframe. Many years ago, even on this kind of furniture, a lock was fitted which only seemed to be there to bang into the key when getting into bed. It is a lot more practical to use a pressure or magnetic-based lock.

7

7/ The engraved flower and
leaves on the front of the drawer cover almost all of its surface. The elegant original solution of putting the turned pommel, is to fit it exactly in the centre of the corolla as if it were just another part of the pattern.

8

8/ The hinges are fitted
on the outside and are bronze with an old-gold finish. They have several good points: they are sturdy and offer a wide opening angle as well as fulfilling a decorative role.

"Bargueño" Decorated Spanish Cabinet.

These pieces of furniture are the most characteristic of the Spanish Renaissance and Baroque epochs, and bear a great Arabian influence *(particularly visible in the decoration based on carved, inlay and marquetry work, metal, precious woods or ivory incrustations).*
This consists of a wooden piece of furniture with lots of drawers and cubby holes. Some people believe that this type of piece originated in the town of Bargas *(Province of Toledo)*, where they were made in times past. The most sought after pieces - and which are kept in museums or palaces of the nobility- were made in the 16th and 17th centuries. They are, however, still made today.
It is a piece of furniture which is essentially used for storing documents or small-sized valuable objects, the piece of furniture can be moved around *(normally on horseback or carriages of that period).*
Originally, therefore, they consisted of what is today considered the upper section which, almost always, had two cast iron handles on the sides. They can be quickly installed on a table top, opened up and put into immediate use. Depending on that table or lower part, also called arch-table, there are several different types *(lyre, bridge, etc.)*, on these, the bargueño itself corresponds only to the upper part though decoration of both is increasingly becoming the same.

The piece of furniture was enriched and took on more sedentary characteristics, until reaching the piece of furniture which is studied on these pages.

With the passing of time, the bargueño gradually acquired other different characteristics while adapting to the services required of it. Now it was no longer for storing things, it now had to work for its living and be used for working at.

Thus, it picked up some features of the more modern bureaus: additions like a surface for writing on, all the contents of the drawers and cubby holes, as well as some larger drawers to better take advantage of the space in the lower section.

1/ Comprised of one single body, the same height as a chest of drawers (the bottom has three drawers plus another one (below) in the base of the piece of furniture). The upper part has two vertical doors which bear the characteristic front composed of small drawers and a central cupboard. In the top (the frieze), there is another drawer like the one in the skirting (even the frontal is decorated the same). At the waist, there is an ample pullout desk top which makes an excellent working surface. The general style of the piece of furniture would seem to date it from around the end of the 19th century (at the height of mahogany, gilded handles and marquetry using motifs encrusted in lighter-hued woods), or faithfully copying a bargueño of that epoch.

2/ This full view of the whole piece of furniture shows the perfect state of preservation of this bargueño, the richness of the pattern on its veneered parts. The inside of the doors and the front of the lower drawers with a beautiful palm pattern (characteristic of mahogany) which covers the three sides of the drawers without breaking up the pattern. This is a piece of furniture built in times when cabinetmakers had reached their highest standards of perfection.

3/ This profile photograph shows the proportions of the piece of furniture with the skirting and frieze covering the two carved and turned columns which decorate the front (on each side). The legs are oblate ball-shaped and made out of the same wood, turned and varnished. The quality of the woods used is outstanding, the piece seen here is the side panel showing the full richness of its grain.

5/ The interior is divided up vertically into three parts: two columns of five drawers apiece (on each side), and a central cupboard. Separating the three bodies of this division are two half columns (pilasters) carved with flutes (dark), and with rings on the top and bottom parts of them. Each group of drawers and the door of the cupboard are decorated with an inlay of light, rectangular-shaped wood. Under this unit, there are a further three small drawers in a row.

4/ Mention has been made before of the patterns on the veneers used, and these are continued on the three drawers in the lower half.
Here, the grain can be clearly seen to continue on the front of the drawers on the top half. The side columns are topped with a carved capital and continue on with a parallepiped on which the frieze on the top half rests. This is raised on the front forming an isosceles triangle (very open) as the top finial of the bargueño.

"BARGUEÑO" DECORATED SPANISH CABINET

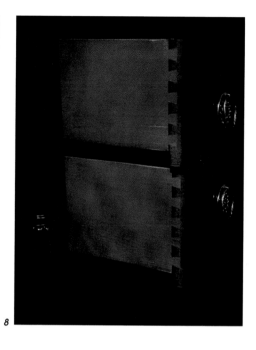

6   7   8

6/ The small drawers and the interior
cupboard of the bargueño are fitted with
button- shaped rounded handles made of
old-gold bronze. These are repeated on the
waist of the piece of furniture to allow easy
extraction of the desktop as well as the
concave drawers in the front of the skirting
and upper half of the piece of furniture.
The three drawers in the lower half have
different handles but still made of the same
material: they are bigger though and are
ring-shaped and decorated in the center
with an engraving and button.

7/ This photograph shows the detail of
the capital of one of the two columns which
flank the front of the piece of furniture.
It is carved in a composite style
(between Ionic and Corinthian) and joins up
with the frieze on the top half via straight
lines and a narrow moulding.
These front corners are mitre cut to offer
suitable siting for the turned and carved
wood columns which they decorate.

8/ Obviously, on a piece of furniture of
the quality seen here on these pages, the
drawers have been assembled using half-
hidden dovetail joins. By the regularity and
perfection of the assembly, it is highly likely
that it has been machine made. In addition,
closer inspection reveals that the handles
and decorations of these drawers are made
in gilded bronze, the decorations linking up
the two elements of the column on the front
corner. The turned part of the circular
section is also decorated vertically with
grooves and waves (the section forms a
flower of sorts).

12/ This
photograph
shows the top
corner of the
back of the
piece of
furniture, as well
as the join
between the
frieze and
cornice of its
sides: solid and
veneered
woods, plus a
perfect finish to
protect them,
even in the
places which
cannot be seen
and which are
left untreated on
some pieces of
furniture.

12

9

10

11

9/ The frieze on the front is triangular-shaped and its stark lines highlight the beauty of the mahogany veneer. Under the mouldings which maintain the continuity of the frieze, this continues on the front concave drawer which is also richly decorated in honey-coloured mahogany.
The perfectly symmetrical motif centred between the two handles, is comprised of two stylised branches with tiny leaves or flowers and some spirals which join up with the central motif -likewise of a vaguely vegetal nature.
The hanging handles of the double door in the top half are also made out of gilded, engraved bronze.

10/ Whatever the angle the photograph may be taken from, the painstaking care taken on the finish stands out, along with the perfect state of preservation of a piece of furniture which, though it may not be exactly an antique, does have the additional plus of being made by craftsmen.
Here, the concave shape of the sides and the front of the skirting can be appreciated. In spite of the this shaping, there is a drawer in the front section, where the inlaid decoration of the top half is repeated.
The four turned legs are thick hooped-shaped with fine rings above and below and firmly fitted into the four corners of the framework.

11/ All the details are carefully executed: hinges, the bolt holding the door closed, etc. This is a beautiful and useful, yet suggestive, piece of furniture: documents, jewellery, mementos... its multiple drawers and cupboards invite one to look for a long lost letter, an intimate diary, maybe something long forgotten by all but the seeker...
These are pieces of furniture which are much more than spaces merely to store things in, they are a slice of history which gains in richness with the passing of generations.

13

13/ It appears almost impossible to achieve such a delicateness as that found in the marquetry work of the top and bottom drawers. With the added difficulty of the concave shape of the surface.
The minuscule slivers of wood grow together to form the most delicate, fragile volutes and the petals of the flowers. This same technique is used to frame the other drawers and the interior of the bargueño.

Tallboy. This kind of tallboy was originally made in two parts: an upper half (*often topped with a carved cornice*), fitted onto another also fitted with drawers and of slightly greater size.
At all events, the decoration (generally columns or carvings stuck to the front corners of the piece of furniture), was conceived as a decoration continued throughout the whole reach of the piece of furniture.

Subsequently, the piece of furniture was made in one piece (*in France they even made a piece of furniture called "semainier" because technically, it had a drawer for each day of the week*).

In some cases, they were used (*like the bargueños*) for storing collections of small artistic objects: porcelain, fans, miniatures, cameos, etc., nature specimens: stones, shells, snail shells, insects or dried plants and flowers. To better keep these valuable, often unique, pieces, each drawer had its own lock or could be locked using an ingenious columnar mechanism which, in one single movement, left all of the drawers locked.

Very often, the top drawer was shorter in height than the others. The piece of furniture detailed on these pages is made out of cherry wood. The structure of the framework and the frames for the drawers are of solid wood. There are four small drawers in the top half with a further six double-sized ones filling the entire piece of furniture. The side panels and top are veneered with cherry wood. This kind of piece of furniture, though having a long history dating back several centuries, is still as practical today in any home as it ever was.
Depending on what it is used to store, clothes or objects - papers, documents, cutlery, etc.- it will always find a place in the lounge, dining room or bedroom, and it was commonplace to find them in men's bedrooms or dressing rooms. Today, it will give presence and prestige to any room it is put in, particularly when it is of the quality of the piece shown here.

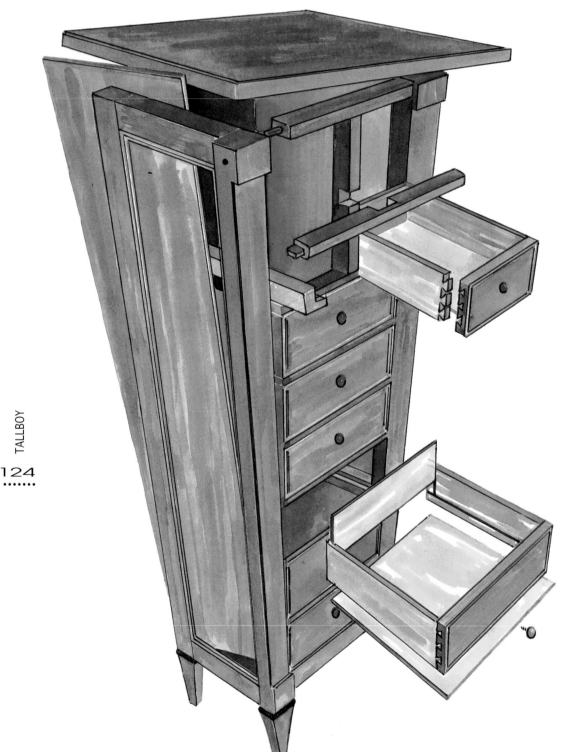

1/ Here, the drawerless piece of furniture can be seen, with the framework holding the drawers laid bare to sight, the two spaces of the top half are divided vertically in two for the four upper drawers. The lateral runners used for sliding the drawers in and out can also be seen.

3/ This foreshortened view shows the quality of the cherry wood with its characteristic reddish moire and beautiful grain. The vertical strip forming the front corner of the framework, is decorated in a square projection (the piece forming the top part of the structure under the moulding of the top), and a delicate piece of engraving and lacquering (a diamond in a darker hue carved into the solid wood). The front of all of the drawers is framed with a plain moulding, of slightly rounded section (half cane), with the corners joined in mitre, also in cherry wood.

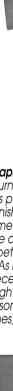

1

2

3

2/ The cherry wood veneered side panel is framed on the straight lines (solid wood) of the structure, underlined above by the plain rounded moulding of the top, underneath by the legs supporting the piece of furniture. They are inverted pyramid-shaped and are fitted on the bottom corners of the framework itself. The light and gradually opening drawers (less to more), form a kind of pyramid, however, here, the quality of the woods used to make their sides can be clearly seen (equal colouring, no knots or defects), as well as the corners joined in dovetail.

5

5/ This photograph shows the whole piece of furniture which, with its sober lines, is painstakingly made and finished without omitting some decorative elements which are commented on (and seen better) in other photographs. As has already been said, this piece of furniture has simple straight lines, but is decorated with some carvings (engraved lines), which are

highlighted in black lacquer, solid cherry wood mouldings and, in the centre of the lower border, a gently patterned small skirt is formed.

4

4/ The side panels meet up with the framework which outlines them with double concave-convex moulding. The corners of said mouldings are mitre-joined. The joins of the framework, however, are made using more solid joins to resist deformation arising from the use and weight of the drawers.

 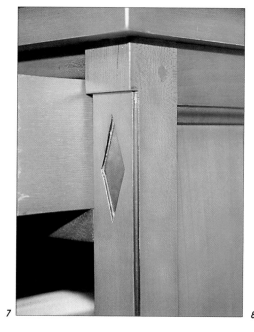 

6

7

8

6/ The quality of the piece of furniture doesn't depend on how many decorative bits or complicated parts it may have: a simple, yet well-executed, design in quality select woods gives a better result and the user will get much greater satisfaction through the years out of it (particularly if they have taken part in building and finishing it). All the solid strips forming the framework of the chest of drawers are simply finished and straight cut (with the corner edges slightly rounded), but the joins which are used to assemble them form part of the decoration itself.

Thus, the frame forming the corner (under the top), appears to be a final extension of the side beams being an offshoot of the vertical, the horizontal beam is fitted in next to this (under the top) as is to logical when building, however, the idea of it jutting out slightly forming a capital of sorts which, on with the lacquered rhomboid, gives it the appearance of a stylised column.

7/ A dark line highlights the edge of the corner and coordinates with the dark lacquering of the rhomboid. The format of the four top drawers is practical and allows them to be used for all kinds of objects. The greater size of the lower draws, on the other hand, makes them better suited for storing clothes, etc., in them.

The front of the drawer has in its centre a simple shiny round knob.

Years ago these were fitted closer to the top edge of the drawer, today they are put smack bang in the centre, thereby favouring a good sliding action when opening the drawer.

8/ It is traditional on all well-made pieces of furniture, for the drawers to be assembled with dovetail joins. Obviously, it is even better when the front and sides are joined using joins of this type -hidden however- the join on the rear is not visible at all. The bottom is fitted into the corresponding groove.

12/ This photograph clearly shows the pin which reinforces the join of the vertical beam with the horizontal one, and the mitred moulding which frames the side panel. The cherry wood stands out owing to its beautiful tonality and the iridescent shine of the grain (after the finish, naturally).

12

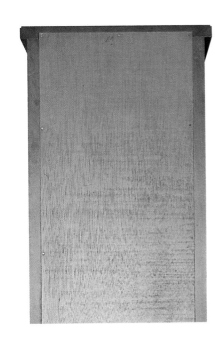

9/ Both the front and rear legs have the same shape (upside down truncated pyramid), which, at the insertion point with the framework, forms a black lacquered curve with the rhomboid engraved on the top part. A similarly engraved fillet frames all of the front beam and the same protrusion is repeated (square) which starts the top part.

10/ A piece of furniture, particularly if it has drawers, cannot be chosen by thinking only on its outward appearance. It is vital that the inside be well built and that the woods used to make the runners for the drawers are in perfect condition and properly levelled. There is nothing quite as disagreeable as trying to open a drawer and finding that it sticks or wobbles when opened. In addition, the inside -remember it is not protected by varnish- is very often prone to be attacked by woodworm (one single hole with the larva inside could cause a plague through the entire piece of furniture).

11/ The rear section of the piece of furniture is formed by a board of thinner wood, and is lightly fixed in place (in this case, with gilded studs), so as to allow the normal play of expansion and dilation undergone by wood (it is, after all, a living material).

13/ View of the top part of the this tallboy with the four drawers open. The unit formed by the fronts bordered entirely by the solid cherry wood moulding and the round knob on the centre of each one, makes the quality and beauty of the piece of furniture clearly obvious (the grain, shine and colour of the well-worked wood, all work to improve the piece and give more authentic results).

TALLBOY

127
·······

Dining room table. Tables are one of the main, and most necessary pieces of furniture used the most in any home, however, a good class table can be a central piece in a lounge, hence the varied and several kinds of table to be found.

When dealing with a style table, made using good woods, properly finished and which, in addition, can be used as a dining table, it takes on a yet greater importance and may even be the piece of furniture which gives character to the decor of that space.

This project studies the construction of an important round table with pedestal, done in the very English classical style and worked in accord with all the mores and traditions of the best cabinetmakers.

The essential part in building a patterned table *(and which is not seen unless the two leaves are opened up and fixed in place as supplements)*, is a kind of box to which the pedestal of the base is firmly fixed to, and which, in the hollow part, houses and allows the two beams which bear the weight of the half boards to be slid out when pulled out from the base and the foldaway leg which is used to support it. This device is called a birdcage mechanism.

There are tables which accumulate all of the decoration on the legs and pedestal, given that when used as a dining table, the top is usually covered by a luxurious tablecloth.

On the piece of furniture shown on these pages, the top is also richly decorated with the set of marquetry done in beautiful mahogany veneers *(sculpted in palms and grains)*.

The illustration clearly shows the different parts which comprise it and how they are fitted together.

1/ The circular table is divided into four parts, each one of which is veneered in American Mahogany (not Cuban which is redder), and the veneers are chosen so that the patterns (the palms and those coming out of the trunk are the most clearly seen), form the decoration. As has already been said, the circle is divided into four parts, each one is, however, veneered with two leaves which reiterate the same pattern, meeting up with two other identical ones situated on the opposing part. In the centre, the patterns of the veneers join up, forming a four-leafed flower of sorts giving a splendid effect. The whole unit is surrounded by a band (delimiting the circle) made using small slivers of finely grained veneer, so placed that the fibre always tends to flow towards the centre and seems to form a ring which frames the rest of the tabletop.

1

2

2/ The skirt of the tabletop is also circular and forms a border slightly smaller than the top and separated from it by a moulding with a series of broad grooves and a half cane. The lower part of this skirt is finished with gentle shallow waves which are repeated all around the circumference and which are decorated with worked motif: two flowers with pointed petals flanked by two complicated acanthus leaves. The relief of this work, like the mouldings and other carved work, is highlighted with a light grey-blue colouring which accentuates the pattern on the more deeply engraved parts.

3/ Some of these tables have the central support resting on three feet, the stability and strength, however, of them is raised when resting on four feet as is the case here. Each of the legs forming the feet are made in solid wood and richly decorated.
Where they are inserted into the central column, they are in cabriolet form and on this curved part, a carving in the form of an acanthus leaf is done. Following the bottom line of these pieces, a fluting highlights their delicate curvatures.
The carving used to decorate them is the same as the one on the four legs. The end of the central column, underneath the union of the four legs, is decorated with a cluster turned out of solid wood with different sized rings (like a peony). The join of each of the legs on the central support is done with a mortise (on the support) and tenon (on the outside of the leg) join.

3

4/ The stylisation of lines of the support accentuates the elegance of this table. The central column alternates very thick parts in its turnings, like a kind of fluted, slightly wreathed melon bulb, with much narrower ones. This variety of diameters can only be strong enough when turned out of one single solid piece of wood. Mention must be made of the finish which, though of a high shine indeed, does not detract from the beauty of the grain, and in fact makes it stand out on both the plain sections as well as the highly worked ones. This part of the support could also be considered a kind of vase, highly typical on this kind of table which combine the support column with the legs in lion's or eagle's claw feet.

4

5/ This photograph shows the full perspective of the base of the table which has been previously described by parts alone. Each of the four legs ends in a rounded shape, decorated yet again with an acanthus leaf whose base wraps around in a spiral and which can be seen on both sides of the leg.

6/ The carving on the top part of the each arm on the conjunction of the four legs with the column of the base, blends together the four joins made there. The spirals of the acanthus leaves hide a very well-made insertion. On the start of each leaf there is another decoration which seems to be a flower (or some very small leaves) with the merest hint of fruits. When the four legs are looked at from the front, the richness and abundance of the carving is unmistakable to the eye, but without actually detracting from the final result of the piece of furniture making it appear quite light and elegant,

thanks to the proportion of its dimensions and the contrast between the carved and plain parts (richly marquetried with the veneers and their patterns).

7/ The great secret of this magnificent table lies in the fact that, aside from having the broad round tabletop which gives space for numerous dining places (up to 6 or even 8 depending on the size of the chairs used to seat diners), it can be extended further. Both halves of the table can be slid and pulled out on the grooves fitted for this purpose under the top, and an additional top is placed on the part left uncovered. Inside the centre which, like all parts not made to be seen, the wood is unvarnished, and two bars can be seen which are though: these are the two auxiliary parts which will allow the open table to retain its stability.

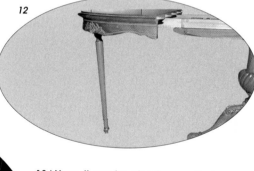

12/ Here, it can be clearly seen that even on the point of maximum load, the beams are sufficiently braced on the central base. The auxiliary leg folds out with the help of a hinge and ensures additional support. The carefully made leg is plain, of round section and tapering down to end at floor level in a simple ball and heel foot which contrasts with the more elaborate feet of the central support.

11/ This photograph perfectly shows the system followed when making the tabletop. The skirt has been fixed to the tabletop and is also divided in two halves. The moulding on the border of the top is of a different wood than that used as the base for its veneering. This is a noble solid wood, the same as the skirt, the support column and legs. The turned auxiliary parts are also varnished and though they appear rather slender, they do give good stability when the table is fully unfolded. Also perfectly visible are the blocks which guide the sliding action of the beams for opening the table up. These blocks are usually made of a harder wood (as the difference in colour suggests) so that they do not wear so much as a result of the continuous friction from repeated slidings.

Five dowel pins and five notches ensure the perfect placing adjustment of the two tabletop halves.

8/ This closeup photograph shows the central part again which is left visible when the two leafs forming the tabletop are separated, and the auxiliary legs, and the base which rests on the support column, etc. Of particular interest to the proper adjustment of the two halves are the small dowel pins which are on one of the leafs and which fit into their corresponding receptacles on the other half of the table. This method ensures a perfectly flat, level tabletop and the join is barely noticeable being visible as a hairline which could very easily be taken for those caused by the tabletop's veneer.

9/ Comparing this photograph with the one on the previous page, the quality of the carving work which exactly repeats the motif worked on the table's skirt can be clearly appreciated, as well as the optical effect caused by the flowers on the border which appear to be inside the vase of

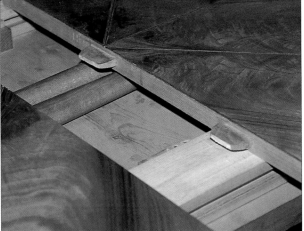

the support column.
The marquetry work done on the tabletop's veneer allows the join between the two adjacent veneers in the centre of the table,

on their edge, however, the join between the tiny pieces is so absolutely perfect that it is indistinguishable from the grain. The quality given this piece by the maker or restorer is blatantly obvious from these small details which are the mark of a piece of furniture's quality.

10/ Another view from a different angle of the table's inside. This was a place where, in times past, some sensitive papers or small jewellery were kept. In this case, the perfect condition of the wood and the absence of dust shows that this is a piece of furniture in perfect condition which has been completely restored quite recently.
It is important that the two parts slide smoothly so that the wooden parts are not damaged or wear or become twisted which would then make opening and closing the table difficult.

13/ This photograph dwells on the beauty of the veneers used to cover the tabletop and the perfect finish which highlights its patterns of palms alternating with areas of woodgrain. In order to get this result, the material had to be very carefully chosen first (it's not always possible to find veneers whose patterns marry up perfectly). Managing to combine them so as to give an attractive and alternating effect is an art in itself. In addition, care must be taken to ensure that the finish of the veneered and solid wood sections all have the same tonality, shine and reflective depth.
All of these points together ensure a quality made piece of furniture, the building of which has to be planned as if it were a unique piece and, even with the advances of modern woodworking machinery today and other facilities, great care and attention to detail from an expert craftsman is still needed (the sensitivity of an artist) if wishing to reach a satisfactory end result.

Chair. A chair in the classical style, though not forming part of a set *(dining room, lounge, etc.)*, if put next to a desk or in a hall, constitutes a key piece in the decor of these spaces. The one studied here bears an unmistakable Chippendale, and that epoch, influence *(18th century)* and style having all of their characteristics: not crosspieces between legs, the front legs done in a marked cabriolet with carvings on the top curvature, upholstered seat *(with the frame visible)*, and the back ones fine and straight. The seat's upholstering, which was originally bordered in petit point, was quite quickly replaced by patterned silk *(with flowers, leaves or fruit like the one here)*. Oak or mahogany wood used, these being the most appreciated materials for chairs owing to their colour, grain, strength and the ease with which they were carved or worked. Carving can be applied or worked in directly on the piece *(as is the case here)*, the openwork back is typical of Rococo-inspired chairs from this famous cabinetmaker who was so famous that he had a style named after him

(Chippendale was inspired by the Gothic, Oriental and Chinese styles).
His models are still reproduced even today. The illustration clearly shows the several parts in detail and how they are assembled to make the chair.

1

2/ The fretwork of the frame on the rear legs can be perfectly seen here *(extension of the back), and the block which strengthens the unit on each corner and gives space for making the joins.*

2

1/ The frame of the seat at the corner has a rounded curve, the acanthus leaf worked leg is inserted just underneath this, the leg has a concave carved on the inside chasing the volutes of the leaves.

3/ This frontal view shows the chair and the elegance of its proportions can be fully appreciated as well as the exquisite openwork pattern of the back's vertical piece. Its top part forms a small central wave underlined by two worked details (a tiny hint of spiral) and two undulations by way of corners on each side.

5/ This photograph shows the ending in small volutes of each side wave which terminate next to the thickest central wave. Mahogany wood is characterised by how well it can be worked and carved.

4/ The sprung upholstered cushion is quite easily removable and allows the seat's framework to be seen.
As is proper on Chippendale style chairs, the chair's front is wider than the back.

7/ This view shows the back of the chair displaying all of the openwork done in stylised waves of the back's central piece. The ends of the front legs terminating in claw and ball can also be seen.

CHAIR

133
••••••

6/ View of the top part (cabriolet) of the front leg with volutes and acanthus leaves adorning it. A narrow concave moulding is carved directly onto the seat's frame.

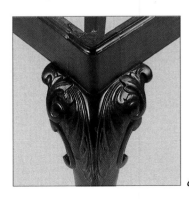

Kitchens. The kitchen is one of the places in the home which has undergone the greatest changes through the passing of time. Life in the country was simpler then: owners and servants met together around the hearth. On the open fire, great pots were cooking resting on the iron grids. However, with the passing of time, kitchens became exclusively the province of servants. This evolution made them much more uncomfortable, rather bleak places. Very often they were places full of cold dark spots which contrasted with the suffocating heat next to the cooking ranges. This situation stayed more or less the same right up to the end of the last century and the beginning of this one. That all changed, however, with the reduction of space in homes in cities and the drop in domestic service, bringing about a radical fall off of that situation. Nowadays, it's not only the housewife who cooks in the kitchen, the whole family now takes part in preparing delicious dishes. The kitchen is very often the central meeting of the family and even their guests. Cooking is a form of culture and deserves a pleasant setting as well as all mod cons and comforts.

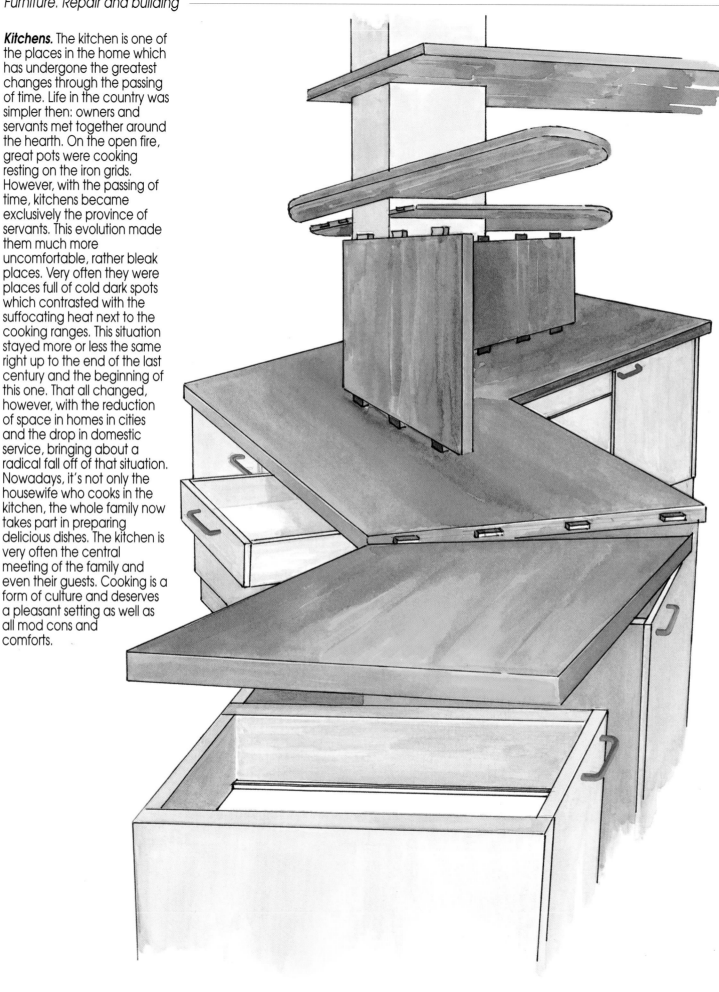

1/ Natural daylight freely enters the kitchen and illuminates the work area. The area set aside for cooking is sited on an islet in the centre, instead of punishing the cook by making them stand facing the wall or cupboards. Set at mid-height and higher, are open shelves which fulfill a useful function as well as being decorative: holding implements, strainers, whisks, bottles and containers, but also plants, jars and books.
This part of the kitchen, without breaking up the continuity, goes on to become the informal dining table. Logically laid out, the top and bottom cupboards and the electrical appliances: refrigerator, freezer, oven, dishwasher, food processor, etc., each element situated in the right place and height for use.

2/ The solid wood chopping block is almost a professional touch, allowing the cutting up and preparation of large pieces of meat, game, etc.
It is placed quite close, but clearly separate from, the cooking area, inviting one to work at ease and with care.
To the front there is a bar from which hang a series of cooking utensils required to be at hand in a kitchen. On the bottom part of this element, a cupboard as a reminder that space in modern day homes is a luxury and must be intelligently used to the full.
Some years ago, a similar kitchen would have been made to order by a team of craftsmen in a workshop and then moved to the house and installed there.

Today though, they are made in modules whose proportions are carefully studied bearing in mind each part in its definitive place. Next, a series of details which help to understand its structure and to appreciate the quality (Miele) of its materials and making.

profoundly researched ergonomic studies to take full advantage of the space available.
One person alone is able to fit

3/ There is a contrast of colour between the dark working top and the rest of the module which makes it stand out, as well as the sink with its accessories and complements: a highly practical wood for cutting up vegetables and then washing them, a mesh drainer over the second sink which is narrower because next to it is a waste disposal unit and a modern monobloc tap which is easily adjustable.

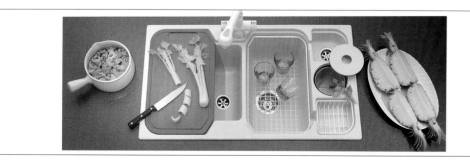

KITCHENS

135
•••••••

4/ To stop the panel of a cupboard coming out because of an asymmetrical overload, each one is fitted with a special fixing device which gives the shelf all of its support at the bottom and holds it at the top.

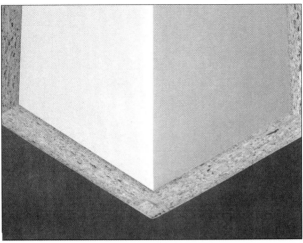

5/ The material chosen for the cupboards is wood but, to make it resistant to humidity and easy to clean, all of its visible surfaces are covered with melamine all over. To make a strong, long-lasting piece of furniture, the corners have been made using a system which guarantees their unalterability and precision of dimensions. The process consists of pressure injecting a synthetic material (in liquid form) through some previously open tubes throughout all of the joins which have to be consolidated.
The liquid penetrates throughout all of the cut surfaces, solidifies and creates a practically indestructible, unalterable, extremely rigid join.

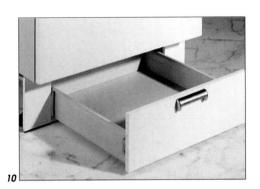

10/ Si interesa aprovechar al máximo el espacio, entre las patas del módulo e incorporado al panel del zócalo, se instala un cajón de chapa de acero lacada que se desliza sobre guías de precisión.
La altura mínima del zócalo ha de ser de 15 cm.

6/ Thanks to the modern metal hinge, simply fitted with screws, doors can be opened to a 110 degree angle. This allows users to work better by being able to put in and take out things from the cupboards.
An automatic system ensures that the hinges are self-adjusting, thereby achieving the perfect opening and closing of the doors. If, at any time, the door has to be removed, it can be taken off and replaced very easily indeed.

11/ Each cupboard module for the lower section of this kitchen is fully enclosed, even on the tops despite the fact of having to be installed under a work top.

The back is also enclosed because this makes the unit totally indeformable and gives a greater degree of protection to everything kept in it.

7/ The height of the skirting can be adjusted because the cupboards are supported on adjustable feet of galvanized steel which are equipped with telescopic elements. To properly locate the module on the floor, the bottom of the foot is made of synthetic and is suitably broad enough.

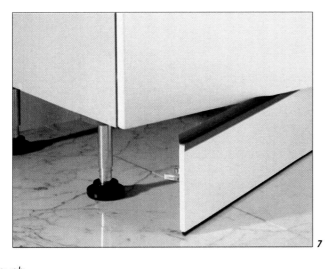

8/ Between the backs and the wall, there is an 8 cm gap which is there to enable cables or pipework and drains to be fitted.

9/ The drawers slide in and out on aluminium runners. This system is designed to last indefinitely, not wear, be maintenance free and easily cleaned. The drawers can be slid in and out very easily indeed, even when they are fully loaded. Thanks to the quick adjustment and change of front parts, they are highly versatile and of variable capacity.

12/ The panels are easy to fit and the feet are very easy to set level. Each panel is fitted with an elastic seal to stop the ingress of water inside.
Each panel is fixed to the feet of the cupboards.

Bathroom. The bathroom is another vital component of the home's most intimate part. Everyone knows that the ideal setup would be to have a private bathroom for each bedroom *(two if the bedroom is a double one)*. Nevertheless, when the bathroom is well-designed and furnished with the right modules, a great deal of space isn't really needed to make it comfortable and can be quite easily shared by the whole family.

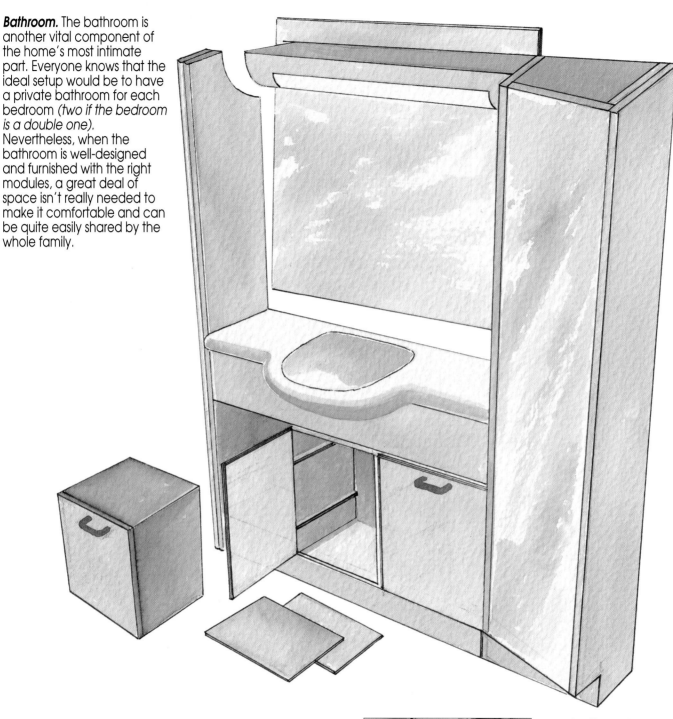

138

1/ Having the towels to hand while also having them where they don't get in the way: this is done here using this highly practical double telescopic towel rail which takes up almost no space at all -it's installed under the side edge of the washbasin's top which forms an overhang to give a wider top.

1

2

2/ Aside from the essential elements: washbasin, shower, bath, etc., there are others which could be considered accessories if it were not for the service they offer and the minimal space they take up thanks to the in-depth ergonomic studies carried out by the Company.
All of them are versatile and easily installed wherever the user likes. This is very much the case with this practical enamelled metal basket kept in the cupboard occupied by the lowest section of this vertical shelving, and which is used for holding clothes prior to them being put in the washing machine.

3/ This washbasin stand with mirror, fitted halogen spots and side cupboard, is comprised of juxtaposed elements which form an elegant unit.
When choosing the different component parts comprising it, bear in mind that, whether it be one single module or a series of them, the panels forming the side skirts of the furniture have to be included in the list of materials to be purchased.
This wide washbasin uses the space underneath it for three cupboards. The top section has a magnificent mirror with three spotlights installed in the soffit which forms the uppermost part.
The use of this mirror is easily combined with the vertical cupboard's door (for towels, etc.) thereby enabling good all round vision. The handles on the drawers and cupboards can be chosen from two very similar models, each made using different materials: in injected resin or lacquered metal. The colour can be chosen from a wide range going from a series of whites and greys to bright or dark colours.

3

5/ One of the best points of this series of modules for bathroom furnishings consists of the variety of skirtings available and how easy it is to fit them.
Their diverse heights, in combination with the sturdy adjustable parts, allow personalised adaptation to each installation's location or height.
There are two finish tonalities available: white and light grey. Each front is held in place by a height adjustable brackets with a good range of adjustment (so that they don't coincide with the same leg as the sides) which are easily fitted by pressing on them. Thus making them easy to fit and remove should the need arise to gain access to fixed installations such as pipework, drains or wiring, etc.

4/ A clean ordered bathroom is always much easier to achieve if the toothbrushes, toothpaste or other personal hygiene products can be put away on their own shelves in containers and receptacles of the right size. The one shown here, is installed on the back of the doors of the cupboards thereby ensuring they are completely out of sight while still being to hand (with the door open, of course), dust free, etc., when the cupboard is closed.
Because of the studied size, this cupboard can be just as easily used for keeping linen, etc. in.
The hinges used to hang the doors are sturdy enough to be able to take this extra weight while giving a wide opening angle to the door, making it easier to access both the cupboard's inside and door.

4

With the support guides fitted, the location of the receptacles can be changed to suit (there are several different types: for toothbrushes, etc., or slightly deeper for bottles or larger sized tubes).

5

cupboard's door held in place by screws included in the accessory's kit and the lid which raises automatically when the door is opened.
To facilitate emptying of the bin, the interior recipient is removable.
The bin can be fitted on either the right or left, is small in size, perfectly suitable for the kind of rubbish it will be used for (17 cm diameter and 24.5 cm high).

6/ This photograph shows a cylindrical bin next to the mirror for throwing away any unwanted bits and pieces: wrapping paper, cottonwool, makeup removal pads, etc. This is installed inside on the
6

INDEX

1/ INTRODUCTION ✿ 9

2/ STYLES
English Renaissance / French Renaissance (Louis XIII) / Spanish Renaissance ✿ 12
Louis XIV and Louis XV / English, Dutch, Low Countries and German furniture / The Baroque in Spain ✿ 14
Louis XVI, Neoclassical, Empire, Consulate / Adam and Hepplewhite, Trafalgar and Queen Victoria ✿ 16
Federal, American Windsor, etc. ✿ 18
Arts & Crafts, Modernism, Cubism, etc. ✿ 20
Rustic furniture ✿ 22
Evolution of styles in different elements ✿ 24

3/ RESTORATION PROJECT (step–by–step)
Rustic chest of drawers ✿ 26

4/ ASSEMBLIES
Classification of joins ✿ 32

5/ RESTORATION AND REPAIR
Treatment for burns ✿ 34
Scratches and marks ✿ 35
Woodworm ✿ 36
Rot ✿ 37
Stains ✿ 38
Repairing hinges ✿ 39
Repairing drawers ✿ 40
Repairing uneven legs ✿ 41
Broken or lost struts ✿ 42
Chair repair (joins) ✿ 43
Repairing tables (winged, etc.) ✿ 44
Repairing joins ✿ 45
Changing glass ✿ 46
Repairing warped wood ✿ 47
Repairing scored wood ✿ 48
Repairing veneers (warped, etc.) ✿ 49
Replacing sections of veneers ✿ 50
Replacing veneers ✿ 51
Replacing broken parts ✿ 52
Removal of opaque paints ✿ 53
Removal of transparent paints ✿ 54
Bleaching and rubbing down ✿ 55

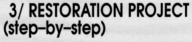

6/ FINISHES AND DECORATIONS

Treatments ✿ 64
Filling pores ✿ 66
Tinting ✿ 67
Transparent protective finishes ✿ 68
Opaque protective finishes ✿ 72
Preparation and priming ✿ 74
Decorative finishes ✿ 75

7/ WORKSHOP AND TOOLS

Workshop and tools ✿ 78
Tools for carving and cutting ✿ 79
Tools for drilling ✿ 80
Tools for gripping and clamping ✿ 82
Tools for sawing ✿ 84
Hammers and screwdrivers ✿ 86
Bits ✿ 87
Tools for rubbing down, scraping and filling ✿ 88
Tools for measuring and sharpening ✿ 90

8/ WOODS

Classification of noble woods and veneers ✿ 94

9/ VARNISHES

Finishes and characteristics of commercial
products ✿ 100

10/ PAINTS

Artisanal imitation of wood ✿ 104
Imitating marble ✿ 106
Imitating porphyry ✿ 108
Imitating Carey ✿ 109

11/ CONSTRUCTION

Display cabinet ✿ 110
Bed ✿ 114
Bedside table ✿ 118
Decorated Spanish
cabinet ✿ 120
Tall dresser ✿ 124
Dining table ✿ 128
Chair ✿ 132
Kitchen ✿ 134
Bathroom ✿ 138

12/ ANALYTICAL INDEX

Index ✿ 140

141
....